VALUE, CAPITAL AND RENT

Also in

By KNUT WICKSELL

Interest and Prices [1936]
Lectures on Political Economy [1934-1935]
Selected Papers on Political Economy [1958]

VALUE, CAPITAL

AND RENT

BY

KNUT WICKSELL, 1851-1926

[1954]

REPRINTS OF ECONOMIC CLASSICS

AUGUSTUS M. KELLEY · PUBLISHERS
NEW YORK 1970

FIRST EDITION 1954

(LONDON: GEORGE ALLEN & UNWIN LTD., 1954)

REPRINTED 1970 BY
AUGUSTUS M. KELLEY · PUBLISHERS
NEW YORK NEW YORK 10001

By *Arrangement With* GEORGE ALLEN & UNWIN LTD.

I S B N 0 678 00652 0
L C N 68 58668

PRINTED IN THE UNITED STATES OF AMERICA
by SENTRY PRESS, NEW YORK, N. Y. 10019

KNUT WICKSELL

Value
Capital
and
Rent

With a Foreword by
Professor G. L. S. Shackle

Translated by
S. H. Frowein

George Allen & Unwin Ltd
RUSKIN HOUSE MUSEUM STREET LONDON

The German original
ÜBER WERT, KAPITAL UND RENTE
was first published in 1893

FOREWORD

to the English translation
by G. L. S. SHACKLE

The great economic theoreticians whose work was completed in the first century and a half from the publication of *The Wealth of Nations* are hardly more than a score. In the compiling of such a list the name of Wicksell would be an early and unquestioned entry, and some might say that he more than any other was the precursor and prophet of modern macroeconomic theory, and provided some of its chief elements a full generation before their power and significance were properly recognized. Wicksell's life coincides to the very year at its beginning and its end with the second half of this first 150 years in the main history of economics: seventy-five years carries us from *The Wealth of Nations* in 1776 to the birth of Wicksell in 1851, and seventy-five years again to his death in 1926.

The early economists beheld a society whose members seemed to fall easily into broad classes according to the parts they played in the economic process. There were those who worked with their hands, those who owned the resources of nature, and those who had accumulated a reserve of more adaptable, mobile or directly enjoyable wealth which made it possible for society to use methods of production affording, as it were, a certain leverage to men's efforts in their endeavour to wrest a living from their surroundings. A prime question which interested these early economists was what principle or mechanism determines the proportions in which the whole product is shared out amongst these classes, the workers, landowners, and capitalists. The idea that men's and nature's work are rewarded with a share of what they jointly produce is easily accepted: but what is the essential nature of the service rendered by an accumulated stock of wealth? How does the availability of such a stock increase the effectiveness with which men's work is applied to nature? And what determines the size which such a stock will at any date attain? The first economist to propose an exact answer to these questions, and thus to construct a theory accounting for the claim of capital owners to a share of the whole produce, and for the precise size of this share, was Böhm-Bawerk; and the essence of his answer was a theory of the role of *time* in the economic process. Böhm-Bawerk was born in the same year as Wicksell, and it is interesting to compare their early careers. Wicksell devoted himself first to mathematics. After taking his first degree in 1872 he seems to have allowed himself a long exploratory period in which postgraduate studies were interrupted by work as a school teacher. He took his final degree in mathematics in 1885, and thus it was not until his thirty-fifth year that he was ready to attack seriously the study of economics. He spent the next five years in England, Germany, Austria and France, and thus was in Austria in those very years when Böhm-Bawerk, whose study of law had led him directly to economics at an earlier age, was completing his theory of capital. Böhm-Bawerk's greatest contribution to economic theory was thus made while Wicksell was still, in economics, in some sense a student. But Wicksell had spent his time in equipping himself with mathematics, and it was this equipment which enabled him to give a more precise and elegant shape to the theory of capital and interest whose main structure had been created by Böhm-Bawerk, and to incorporate it into a general theory of the inter-dependent mutual determination of income shares on the principle of marginal productivity. The result was Wicksell's first book, which appeared in 1893 under the title *Über Wert, Kapital und Rente*, and which has in the following pages been for the first time translated into English.

The use of the marginal analysis to explain the prices of the factors of production was achieved by several economists independently of each other, notably by Marshall, J. B. Clark and Wicksteed as well as Wicksell. The thinking on marginal lines which Marshall embodied in his *Principles* was begun before 1870, but *The Principles of Economics* was not published till 1890. J. B. Clark's *The Distribution of Wealth* was not published till 1899, but Clark had been working on its substance for a decade before publication. Wicksell is said to have conceded the claim that it was Wicksteed who, in his *Essay on the Co-ordination of the Laws of Distribution*, published in 1894, first showed that, under some restrictive but still interesting definitions and assumptions, if each engaged unit of each factor of production is paid the marginal product of that factor, the whole produce will be exactly exhausted without surplus or deficit. But this proposition is at least implicit in *Über Wert, Kapital und Rente*. Thus Wicksell's first great contribution to economic theory used the method nowadays called comparative statics, whereby we study the ultimate and supposedly stable consequences themselves of some change of the governing conditions, rather than the mechanism or process by which those consequences are brought about. But Wicksell had in a supreme degree the urge and the power to synthesize, to see economic theory as a comprehensive unity where every important economic pheno-menon must find an explanation at least compatible with that of every other such phenomenon. His mathematical training, or perhaps the natural aptitude and proclivity of mind that had led him to seek such a training, must have been a powerful factor in this drive towards synthesis. *Über Wert, Kapital und Rente* was a first step, for it brought time, in some aspects at least, into the previously timeless theory of value and income distribution. When Wicksell began to work on the explanation of what determines the general level of money prices and of how the changes of this level come about, he did not turn his back on the theory of the 'real' economic forces and start afresh, but on the contrary the theory of the 'real' interest rate, which he had developed in *Über Wert, Kapital und Rente* on Böhm-Bawerkian foundations, became a central and essential element. And this theory of the general price level turned out to be one of the chief sources of inspiration for later theorists of the business cycle and thus an integral part of a still more inclusive conception.

Wicksell's work was like a mountain from whose flanks divergent streams run down and bring fertility to widely separated fields, only to merge again later into a single broad river. For the fiercest and most exciting battle of economic theory in the first half of the twentieth century was that fought in the middle thirties between the adherents of Professor Hayek's over-investment theory of the business cycle, on the one hand, and Lord Keynes and his lieutenants on the other. No two theories, it seemed at that time, could be more directly opposed to each other in method and conclusions. Yet in both of the books from which the controversy started, Keynes's *Treatise on Money* which appeared in 1930 and Professor Hayek's *Prices and Production* which was published in 1931, Wicksell's name was prominent and the power and insight of his analysis acknowledged.[1] And the solution of this paradox, as we can now discern it, is no less surprising: Lord Keynes was setting out the theory of under-employment and Professor Hayek that of over-employment; these were in a fundamental sense two sides of the same theory, one of them describing what happens when effective demand for productive resources is less than the available resources and the other explaining the mechanism of boom, crisis, and collapse which result from an attempt to use more resources than there are. The flat contradiction in which the two theories seemed to confront each other was illusory; they were no more contradictory than the two statements, that if a stone is denser than water it will sink, and if a cork is less dense than water it will float. The basis of Professor

---

[1] 'There remains, however, one outstanding attempt at a systematic treatment, namely Knut Wicksell's *Geldzins und Güterpreise*, published in German in 1898, a book which deserves more fame and much more attention than it has received from English-speaking economists. In substance and intention Wicksell's theory is closely akin . . . to the theory of this *Treatise*.'
J. M. Keynes, *A Treatise on Money*, Vol. I, p. 186.

Hayek's theory was the Austrian theory of capital, which Böhm-Bawerk had founded and Wicksell had interpreted and refined. Professor Hayek showed how the power of the banking system to create money and thus, through an 'artificially' low market rate of interest, delude the economy into thinking that it had a larger potential flow of real investible resources than in fact it had, could lead to a crisis where people might find themselves rich in half-constructed railways but starving for lack of today's dinner; and it is precisely the mechanism and nature of the ultimate dependence of our choice of methods of production upon our available reserves of sustenance that Wicksell, following Böhm-Bawerk and in essence the wage-fund theorists, is concerned with in *Über Wert, Kapital und Rente*. The banks' power to create money? But this is also what Keynes was concerned with in his *Treatise*, and again what Wicksell had been concerned with in his famous book *Geldzins und Güterpreise*, published in 1898, in which the essential and many-fold importance of *time* in the economic process is made the king-pin of a fundamental synthesis.

In the early 1870's Jevons, Menger and Walras had independently and almost simultaneously created the marginal utility theory of value, which explains how the ratios in which different goods exchange for one another are determined by the balancing of marginal subjective desires. But there was one startling omission from the list of things whose value in terms of each other could be thus accounted for. The subjective theory of relative prices depends on the principle of diminishing marginal utility; utility, that is to say, for purposes of consumption. But *money* is not consumed, it is merely exchanged or stored, its utility must therefore be of quite a different kind from that of consumable goods, and its value in terms of these goods must require some different principle for its explanation. In Wicksell's own words 'It is of no consequence whatever to a purchaser that he has to pay more for one commodity provided he can be certain of himself obtaining a correspondingly higher price for some other commodity.'[1] The general level of absolute or money prices was, in fact, left unexplained by the marginal utility theory of value, and some other account had to be given of it. Until the appearance of *Geldzins und Güterpreise* the prevailing explanation was the Quantity Theory, whose crude arithmetical argument presents a striking contrast, as Professor Hicks has pointed out,[2] with the subtlety of the theory of value. The Quantity Theory assumes that the frequency with which money

[1] *Interest and Prices*, by Knut Wicksell, translated by R. F. Kahn (Macmillan and Co. Ltd., London 1936) p. 39.
[2] See 'A suggestion for simplifying the theory of money,' by J. R. Hicks, *Economica*, New Series, No. 5

units change hands, when averaged over all the money units in existence, is fairly constant through time, and from this deduces that the total money value of transactions per unit of time is proportional to the number of money units in existence. Thus so long as the size of the stream of goods being bought and sold remains in some sense unchanging, the general level of prices will depend on the Quantity of Money, that is, on the number of money units in existence.

Wicksell by no means rejected the Quantity Theory *in toto*, but he was disturbed by its dependence, in its classical form, on the assumption of a constant velocity of circulation of money: 'The Quantity Theory,' he says,[1] 'is *theoretically* valid so long as the assumption of *ceteris paribus* is firmly adhered to. But among the "things" that have to be supposed to remain "equal" are some of the flimsiest and most intangible factors in the whole of economics—in particular the velocity of circulation of money, to which, in fact, all the others can be more or less directly referred back.' How strongly these words suggest Lord Keynes's later pre-occupation with the elusive essence of money and its recalcitrance to a purely mechanical, non-psychological analysis. Ricardo had, of course, believed that there was an intimate and indeed an obvious connection between *changes* in the quantity of money, *changes* in the general level of prices (or its inverse, the value of money) and the *level of the interest-rate*. A willingness of the banking system to increase continually the outstanding amount of its loans or of its note issue could express itself, and become effective, only by a low rate of interest. As soon as the outflow of extra money into public circulation ceased, prices of goods would soon adjust themselves to this new larger quantity of the circulating medium; at these new higher prices, the quantity of money would no longer be *in effect* any greater than before, and the interest-rate would accordingly return to its former level. But Wicksell, though agreeing with Ricardo's conclusion, did not think that Ricardo had penetrated deeply enough into the mechanism by which interest, the quantity of money, and the price-level are connected with each other. For what, he asked, is a *low* rate of interest? By what criterion do we judge when the rate of interest is low? By comparison with *what* is it low?

Wicksell found the answer by looking back at that branch of economic theory which had been his earliest concern, and which he had expounded in *Über Wert, Kapital und Rente*, the theory of capital. The more highly articulated, specialized and elaborate the system of equipment becomes through which men apply their effort to their natural environment, the larger the ultimate reward to a given effort, but to carry the elaboration from a given degree to a

[1] *Interest and Prices*, p. 42.

still higher one implies the foregoing of, say, N units of consumable output which would have been available in year T in exchange for the prospect of an extra m units per year in perpetuity, beginning in year $T + 1$. The ratio $\frac{m}{N}$ then represents, nearly enough, what Wicksell called the *natural rate of interest*. It is a measure of the 'worthwhileness,' at any stage of the development of the economy's total assemblage of productive equipment, of adding one more 'unit' to that equipment. How are such units to be defined? In making such an addition to their total equipment the people composing the economy are, in effect, *postponing* the consumption of some of the output which their current input of productive services entitles them to consume. The average time elapsing between the moment when a dose of work or of the services of nature is put into the productive process, and the moment when the dose of consumable product attributable to that dose of work comes out, is thus lengthened, and this average time, Böhm-Bawerk's 'average period of production,' can serve as a measure of the size of the total capital equipment. A balanced assemblage of such capital equipment,[1] comprising tools, machines, buildings, flocks and herds, growing crops, forests, mines, libraries, transportation systems, and indeed the whole material frame of civilized life, is like a great reservoir into which human effort has been poured and from which the means of living can be drawn off. The metaphor of a reservoir will serve to illustrate the meaning and use of the average period of production. If a heavy shower of rain falls on an actual reservoir on a particular day, some of this rainwater will flow out for use on that same day, but a large proportion will remain for many days or weeks mixed with the rest of the reservoir's contents, and it would indeed be possible to describe the size of the reservoir by saying how long, on the average, with a *given* outflow, each drop of water that enters it remains in it. The natural rate of interest, then, is a measure of the strength of the inducement to increase the average period of production; and in a given set of other circumstances, the numerical value of the natural rate, the percentage $\frac{m}{N}$, will be a decreasing function of the length of the average period of production. But these 'other circumstances' are, of course, just as important, in determining the natural rate of interest, as the average period of production itself is. In Wicksell's own words:[2] 'The natural rate is not fixed or

---

[1] In *Über Wert, Kapital und Rente* Wicksell treated highly durable goods as 'Rentengüter,' that is, goods whose durability renders them economically akin to the self-maintaining forces of nature.

[2] *Interest and Prices*, p. 106.

unalterable in magnitude. . . . In general, we may say, it depends on the efficiency of production, on the available amount of fixed and liquid capital, on the supply of labour and land, in short on all the thousand and one things which determine the current economic position of a community; and with them it constantly fluctuates.' Now it was this *natural rate of interest* by comparison with which, at any time, the rate of interest charged by the banks for money loans could be said to be high or low. 'Now let us suppose,' says Wicksell,[1] 'that the banks and other lenders of money lend at a different rate of interest, either lower or higher, from that which corresponds to the current value of the natural rate of interest on capital. The economic equilibrium of the system is *ipso facto* disturbed. If prices remain unchanged, entrepreneurs will in the first instance obtain a surplus profit . . . over and above their real entrepreneur profit or wage. This will continue to accrue so long as the rate of interest [on loans of money] remains in the same relative position. They will inevitably be induced to extend their business in order to exploit to the maximum extent the favourable turn of events, . . . As a consequence, the demand for services, raw materials, and goods in general will be increased, and the price of commodities must rise.'

In this brief and simple-seeming passage we have the epitome of Wicksell's great theoretical achievement: to have shown that the link between the quantity of the circulating medium and the general price-level can be explained by reference to those same principles of individual maximization of advantage which underlie the theory of relative prices and income shares. The classical Quantity Theory was a mere piece of arithmetic masquerading as an explanation, for it did not show by what mechanism and through what human motives, decisions and conduct the change in the price-level would come about; and without a reference to human motives and conduct there can be no understanding of price.

The value of the contribution which an economic theoretician has made to his subject is not to be assessed by means of the questions: Are the analytical tools that he invented still in use? Do we still think along precisely the lines that he laid down? The fact that ships now sail through the Suez and the Panama Canals does not lessen the importance of the voyages of Vasco da Gama and Magellan. The steam locomotive, perhaps, is nearly obsolete, but it has played its part in building up the material resources and the technical knowledge of modern society. Amongst the concepts for which a tool of rather different meaning and character has nowadays been substituted is Wicksell's natural rate of interest, but its disappearance from our vocabulary can never alter the truth

---

1 *Interest and Prices*, p. 105.

that a large part of the route to our present understanding was cleared by Wicksell's efforts. Wicksell's concern was with the mechanism of a continuous rise in the general price-level going on while real resources were all the time fully employed, and not in any sense with that of the growth of real output beginning in conditions of heavy under-employment. In the 1930's, however, it was, of course, upon this latter problem that attention was concentrated, and in the Keynesian theory of employment, instead of a natural rate of interest determined by *technical* conditions as these work or would work in a state of *full employment*, a natural rate determined, that is to say, independently of the prevailing level of employment and of the supply-prices of capital goods which vary with the level of employment, a natural rate which thus stands immovable while the money rate conforms or fails to conform with it, attention was directed instead to the marginal efficiency of capital, defined as that rate of discount which, when applied to the series of expected net earnings of pieces of capital equipment, yields for these pieces a 'present value' equal to their current supply-price. The marginal efficiency of capital, thus defined, is, of course, a function of the supply-prices of capital goods, and will fall in numerical value as these prices are pushed upwards, along a rising supply-curve, by an increase in the level of net investment. So long as business men's valuations of equipment stand above the supply-price of this equipment, they will have an incentive to increase the quantity of it that they order per unit of time; through this increase in the pressure upon the equipment-producing industries, the price of equipment will be raised to the point where the marginal efficiency of capital is brought to equality with the market rate of interest on loans of money. The differences between this theory of the determination of the size of the net investment flow, that is, the determination of the pace of net enlargement or improvement of the economy's equipment, on the one hand, and Wicksell's theory of the consequences of inducing enterprisers, through an unnaturally low interest rate, to seek to expand their operations when all real resources are already fully employed, are clear and striking and may be thought to set the two theories far apart from each other. Yet both theories clearly belong to the same family, and Wicksell's conception, of a mechanism in which the peculiar properties of bank-created money can work through the interest rate and the inducement to expand enterprise to generate a self-propelling cumulative process, entitles him to be considered the founder of that *unified* theory of money, employment, and the business cycle, to which Sir Dennis Robertson, Professor Hayek, Lord Keynes and many others later gave such a complex and dramatic evolution.

* * *

The translation here offered of Wicksell's *Über Wert, Kapital und Rente* has been made by Mr. Stephen Horst Frowein. The endless care which he has lavished upon the work, his natural gift for the subtleties of language, his qualifications as an economist who graduated at the University of Bonn and studied later at the University of Leeds, and the felicity of his English prose style, have produced a translation whose excellence must, I think, be apparent to every reader, and must surely astonish those who have any practical acquaintance with the difficulties of such a task. One may fairly claim that this book, which was written by a Swede in German, here reads as though it was the original work of an Englishman. An admirable tribute has thus been paid by the translator and his publishers to the memory of a very great economist.

The value to economists and historians of economic thought of this first English version of Wicksell's earliest book has, I think, been greatly enhanced through the generosity of Mr. Arne Amundsen of the Universitetets Socialøkonomiske Institutt of Oslo, who, with a kindness that we most warmly appreciate, has allowed his complete bibliography of Wicksell's published works to be printed for the first time as an Appendix to this volume.

G. L. S. SHACKLE

University of Liverpool
August 28, 1953

TRANSLATOR'S NOTE

I wish to take this opportunity of thanking Professor A. J. Brown for having first drawn my attention to the need for an English translation of Wicksell's *Über Wert, Kapital und Rente*.

I also desire to acknowledge the generous help of my friend Mr. H. G. Tupper, who gave unstintingly of his time and expert knowledge of the English language and without whose assistance it would scarcely have been possible for me to undertake this task.

A debt of the deepest gratitude which I cannot well express I owe to Professor G. L. S. Shackle, not only for his introduction, but also for his countless valuable suggestions after most carefully reading the entire MS. Although I am solely responsible for any blemishes and mistakes, it is only fair to say that any merits which this translation may possess are in a very large degree due to his exact scholarship and to his friendly corrections of my rendering which I adopted throughout.

S. H. F.

CONTENTS

AUTHOR'S PREFACE

The rough outline of this little work, or rather the first impulse which led me to write it, was provided by a few popular lectures delivered by me in Stockholm several years ago, in which I tried to present the fundamentals of the modern theory of value and of Böhm-Bawerk's theory of capital, which had just then been published.

The first of these lectures, which deals with the older theories of value, I have used here in substantially unchanged form as an *introduction*. Although it was not originally intended for a public trained in this subject, and will probably still show traces of this, I hope that it will also be of some interest to the circle of readers which I address here. It consists of an attempt to evaluate the classical theory of value as it left Ricardo's hands—its merits, especially when compared with the later theories of the 'harmony economists' and the socialists, and its defects. At a time when it has almost become a fashion to speak of Ricardo in disparaging terms, it may be permissible to emphasize once again the unquestionable merits of this acute thinker. I can by no means share Wieser's opinion,[1] that Ricardo's works exhibit 'the great youth of economic science.' On the contrary; as I see it, his presentation, compared with the vagueness of many later schools, the superficiality of a Carey or a Bastiat and the 'Hegelian' darkness—and conceit— of Karl Marx, is distinguished by what I should choose to call its masculine features. He appeals to the understanding of his readers instead of to their emotions.

Next, I have tried in the *first chapter* to present the fundamentals of the more recent theory of value, following Walras's methods. There is no need to deal in great detail with the principles and the philosophical basis of the modern interpretation of these phenomena, for this part of the subject can be expected to have become the common property of the learned world through the works of the Menger school and especially through Böhm-Bawerk's extremely lucid presentation.[2]

[1] *Der natürliche Wert*, preface, p. IV.
[2] 'Grundzüge der Theorie des wirtschaftlichen Güterwerts' (in *Conrads Jahrbücher*, 1886).

However, the same can scarcely be said of the mathematical treatment of economic problems introduced by Jevons and Walras. And this, if I am not mistaken, is partly due to certain defects of the works concerned, as well as to other circumstances. Jevons's presentation is, I admit, uncommonly clear and stimulating, but he has not penetrated sufficiently deeply into the nature of the matter at just the decisive points. His famous 'equations of exchange' are founded on the assumption of a kind of collective marginal utility of a group of exchanging persons—a concept of which it is impossible to form any clear idea. The simplicity of the formulae arrived at in this way is therefore merely an apparent simplicity. In just the same way he deals with the important question of the exchange of three (or more) commodities, without taking into account the *correlativity* of the reciprocal proportions of exchange which necessarily results when trade is completely free; and consequently his result in reality only covers a very special case, rarely occurring and certainly not thought of by him.

Walras's work is in this respect absolutely faultless; but his presentation suffers from an extremely cumbersome terminology, which makes his book rather laborious reading—even for mathematically trained readers. His German follower Launhardt, a skilled mathematician, presents Walras's principles in a simpler and more lucid form; but for the rest, Launhardt's work presents a striking example of the way in which a mathematical treatment of economic problems ought *not* to be carried out.

The considerable number of 'propositions' put forward by him is arrived at partly through economic reflections of very doubtful value. Partly—in so far as they are founded on correct principles—they presuppose everywhere the applicability of certain approximating formulae which at best prove correct in special cases, but cannot possibly prove correct—or even approximately correct—generally.

It was my task here, with reference to the above-mentioned works, to present the main features of the mathematical doctrine of value in the most easily understandable form possible, by setting out from the simplest assumptions and proceeding to the more complicated cases; avoiding, however, any diffuseness in the formulae.

One point which I have made a special effort to elucidate is concerned with the question of the so-called economic gain by exchange. H. H. Gossen, the predecessor of Jevons and Walras, had laid down the rule, which in itself is quite correct, that 'for a maximum of value to arise, the last (received or surrendered) particle' of each of the commodities must, after the exchange has taken place, have the same utility or value *for both exchanging persons*. If this were also the case *under conditions of free trade* (which Gossen certainly does not assert), then it would indeed be the remarkable attribute of free exchange to call forth the greatest possible economic gain or total satisfaction. This, however, is not the case. The fundamental law of exchange asserts, not that the marginal utility of each commodity by itself is the same for both parties to the exchange, but that the *ratio* of the marginal utilities of the two commodities is the same for both parties. The former condition, to be sure, includes the latter, but the latter does not include the former. Walras, who, with Jevons and C. Menger, discovered the real law of exchange, has nevertheless in several passages of his writings, when speaking of the profit arising from exchange, given a wrong or at least misleading formulation to the result of the theory. He says amongst other things:[1]

'L'échange de deux marchandises entre elles sur un marché régi par la libre concurrence est une opération par laquelle tous les porteurs, soit de l'une des deux marchandises, soit de l'autre, soit de toutes les deux, peuvent obtenir la plus grande satisfaction de leurs besoins compatible avec cette condition de donner de la marchandise qu'ils rendent et de recevoir de la marchandise qu'ils achètent dans une proportion commune et identique.'

Taken literally, this is obviously not true. A uniform price or proportion of exchange of both commodities could also come about in other ways than by free competition—for instance, by prices fixed by the authorities or by agreements on the part of one or the other party to the exchange; and it is quite possible that the party concerned would obtain thereby a profit higher than can be obtained in the case of free competition. It cannot be proved even generally—as Launhardt (who has at other times engaged in the critical discussion of this very problem) oddly enough asserts—that the profit of both parties together must become greater in the case of free competition than in

---

[1] *Éléments d'économie politique pure*, 2nd Ed., 10th Lec., p. 121.

the case of any other exchange transacted *at a uniform price*, though this will usually be the case.

These repeated errors in regard to a question which seems especially suitable for mathematical treatment, could give rise to doubt about the usefulness of this method. The fault, however, does not lie in the calculation, which was correctly carried through by Walras as well as by Launhardt, but in the formulation of the result of the calculation; and though the use of mathematical symbols is not an infallible way of avoiding errors, at least it offers the advantage that these errors cannot long remain undiscovered.

I have not taken into consideration the well-known work by Auspitz and Lieben, *Untersuchungen über die Theorie des Preises*, except in a single passage, where I try to refute their attack, unfounded in my opinion, on a proposition of Walras. I am by no means unaware of the merits of these authors, especially in regard to the question of the consumption of goods, still so little discussed. I can only regret that they wished to be quite independent in their investigations, instead of following earlier works on the same subject; with the result that it becomes really difficult to decide how far previously accepted results are confirmed or refuted by their work. Interesting also is the theoretical parallelism between consumption and production, between 'the way of producing and the way of living' (*Betriebs- und Lebeweise*), which they strove to establish. However, it is open to doubt whether this parallelism will prove fruitful scientifically. They have left completely untouched the important question of the role of capital in production.

Though the first chapter of my book will offer only a little of what is new to experts in the literature of the subject, I may perhaps call the contents of the *second chapter* more my own intellectual property. An exact, mathematical treatment of the theory of capital interest has, to be sure, already been attempted by Jevons and Walras. Jevons's treatment, however, is rather superficial. Although one can hardly accuse the author of a *wrong* interpretation, as Böhm-Bawerk does, he at any rate leaves important aspects of the matter out of consideration.

In this connexion Walras has made an extremely praiseworthy attempt to summarize the phenomena of the production of goods in actual equations, according to the same principles as the phenomena of exchange before. According to him, economic production would be nothing else but an exchange between the products and the 'productive services' of labour, land and capital; and in the last instance production would even be an exchange between these productive services themselves. In this field Walras's investigations probably belong to the most abstract and difficult ever written about economic questions, and it is no easy task to estimate exactly the importance of his assumptions concerning these questions, and the correctness of his conclusions.

I have, however, been able to convince myself that his theory of production suffers from a fundamental mistake connected with his old-fashioned and one-sided interpretation of the concept of capital, which could only be removed by a thorough revision of his presentation. I have therefore left Walras at this point, in order to side with the more recent theory of capital, the beginnings of which we already find in Jevons, but which was fully developed in Böhm-Bawerk's outstanding work, *Positive Theorie des Kapitals*.

My agreement with the last-mentioned author is, however, not a complete one. Already in the matter of the correct definition of the concept of capital I have raised several objections to his view, and especially to the distinction which he makes between social and private capital. These I submit to the thinking reader, without, however, flattering myself that I have removed all the difficulties which beset this much-discussed subject.

On the other hand, I think that Böhm-Bawerk's main formula for the explanation of interest—that interest is an agio or premium which arises from exchange between present and future goods—is quite correct and appropriate. But I cannot give to it such a decisive significance compared with the older theories as was probably required by the author himself. Its applicability is shown, it seems to me, more in the theory of capital *formation* than in the real theory of interest. As I see it, these two questions—the question of the origin of capital interest and that of the origin of interest-bearing capital itself—however closely they are related, must in theory be first of all treated separately, just as, for instance, the theory of exchange is separated from the theory of production, though in reality exchange and production are almost always dependent on each other. If one does this, or what comes to about the same: if one takes as a fundamental—and simplest—hypothesis the *stationary* economy in which capital and the other economic factors can be thought of as an approximately unalterable sum, then some of the most important of Böhm-Bawerk's objections to the older theories[1] lose their significance, and the theory of productivity as well as the Use theory can then be applied to the investigation of the actual phenomena of interest quite as appropriately as his own—and in some respects even more so.

It is characteristic that Böhm-Bawerk himself, in the last chapter of his *Positive Theorie*, where he deals with the important problem of the determination of the level of interest in the market, follows throughout the older productivity theory of Thünen. The question of exchange between present and future goods no longer arises here; or, more correctly speaking, the attempt of the author to explain the phenomena in question from this point of view as well, proves a failure; not because his principle is faulty, but simply because, when this mode of explanation is adopted, the matter looks considerably more complicated than Böhm-Bawerk seems to have believed.

The greatest merit of his book lies, it seems to me, in the further continuation of the theory advanced by Thünen and Jevons. Following the precedent of the last-mentioned author, he conceives the true role of capital in production as merely an advance of means of subsistence which makes possible the adoption of longer, but more fruitful, processes of production. In this way the *length of the period of production* is for the first time introduced into the subject as an independent concept, which will presumably prove extremely fruitful.

That one so modern and so free from prejudice in his outlook as Ch. Gide can still only half approve this entire mode of interpretation, shows how new it in fact is. He remarks[2] that an economic undertaking—for instance, the boring-through of the Isthmus of Panama—does not start with the accumulation, once for all, of a quantity of provisions which will suffice for about eight or ten years. Certainly not! But surely the means

---

[1] I say explicitly: Objections to the theories. As regards their manner of *presentation* Böhm-Bawerk may often be right; I have certainly no desire to belittle the great merit of the critical part of his investigations either.

[2] *Principes d'Économie Politique*, 2nd ed., p. 143 ff.

of subsistence of the workers (and of the owners of the land, too, if the landed property is rented by the capitalists) refer to a point in time which lies, *on an average*, not at the beginning of the period which must elapse before the completion of the products, but about half-way through this period. Only the most superficial consideration could draw from the circumstance that finished goods come upon the market almost every moment (owing to the fact that in reality different business undertakings run side by side and interlock), the completely wrong, but unfortunately so common, conclusion that the workers are maintained not by capital but by the proceeds of production itself.

Böhm-Bawerk's treatment of the problem is, especially in the last chapter of his book already referred to, in essence a mathematical one, although he avoids the use of mathematical symbols on principle and tries to get along by setting down hypothetical series of numbers in tabular form. This method, which might perhaps have some advantage for readers without a previous knowledge of mathematics, is, however, in several respects, a rather clumsy one, and has probably led the author himself to wrong conclusions. In place of his tables I use algebraic expressions and a suitable, and very simple, geometrical construction. By this means, it seems to me, the whole theory gains considerably in simplicity and perspicuity, and the content of the rules is increased; for, as can be seen, the expressions remain unaltered if, instead of the capitalists, one conceives the workers themselves as entrepreneurs, or thinks of the function of both as being partly united in the same persons; whilst they immediately cease to be valid if, instead of completely free competition, one takes as their basis some other assumption—for instance, the economic banding together of the capitalists or workers, etc.

At the same time, I have succeeded in carrying through a *generalization* of the equations concerned. By this means the *services of the land*, which Böhm-Bawerk did not take into consideration, are incorporated in the theory. Although this extension was pretty obvious, I may perhaps draw the attention of the interested reader to my formulae (20)–(24), which are relevant in this connexion; for as I see it, the relationship between the main economic factors, labour, land and capital, is here for the first time exactly stated. This, under given assumptions, makes possible the theoretical determination of wages, rent and capital interest.

I have no better way of showing that a mathematical treatment, or rather the mode of thought and expression of the infinitesimal calculus, was wholly appropriate, indeed almost unavoidable here, than by adducing for purposes of comparison the treatment of the same problems in Wieser's well-known book *Der natürliche Wert*.

Wieser suggests that in order to find out the share of the total profit or, as he expresses it, 'the productive contribution' of the different productive factors, one should place side by side a sufficient number of different but actually occurring combinations of the same productive elements, so as to be able to estimate according to the principle of simultaneous equations the proportion of each element which is everywhere equal, from the known value of the total sum. For instance, 'to reduce the entire number of expressions which offer themselves to the shortest possible form,' one would obtain, for three means of production x, y and z, 'the following equations:

$$x + y = 100$$
$$2x + 3z = 290$$
$$4y + 5z = 590$$

where $x = 40$, $y = 60$ and $z = 70$.'

Now it is clear that, proceeding in this way, however great the number of the equations may be, we shall learn nothing more than we knew already, namely that when competition is free the remuneration for, or the share in the proceeds of, one and the same 'means of production' must be approximately the same in all transactions. The above equations tell us this and nothing more, as can easily be seen. If, therefore, Wieser meant by his expression 'productive contribution' (*produktiver Beitrag*) merely the remuneration actually obtained from the different factors of production—the reward for common labour, the rent for land of equal quality, the average capital interest, and so on—then he has stated a true, but self-evident rule. If he meant something else, then his 'solution' must *a priori* be declared false.

In either case his method gives absolutely no information concerning what we really want to know, namely how and why the participation of different elements of production receives precisely such and such a reward.

In order to discover this, we must, instead of looking at the quantities in question themselves, consider rather their changes (as, by the way, Wieser himself points out later, but with little consistency); that is to say, we must approach the subject from the standpoint of the differential calculus.

This means that, if we conceive the total proceeds of production as a real (stable) function of the participating factors of production (which must be regarded as approximately true),[1] then obviously thrift requires that each factor shall be employed in such quantities that the falling out of a small portion of this quantity would diminish the result of the production by an amount equal to the share in the proceeds which belongs to this quantity. That is to say, so long as this condition is not fulfilled, it will always be more remunerative for the entrepreneur of the business, whoever he may be, to employ either more or less of the elements of production in question.

Mathematically expressed, this means that the share in the proceeds of the different factors of production must be proportional to the partial derivative of the above-mentioned function in respect of the factor in question as variable; and in this simple formula lies indeed the true solution of the problem, provided that at the same time the special position of capital as an element in production is sufficiently considered.

With the help of the rules thus stated I am at last in a position to consider afresh the problem of the exchange of goods, taking production into account. Setting out from the simplest typical case, I suppose first two economic units existing side by side, each with a given amount of capital, labour and natural resources, but each producing only one commodity, which will later be exchanged with the commodity produced by the other unit. Next, both these economic units are conceived by me as uniting in a single unit.

Lastly, I have tried to indicate how the equations of production and exchange which apply to this particular case must

1 It is true that if changes in the individual economies occur, they can for the most part only do so erratically. However, due to the law of large numbers, this does not mean that the resulting changes cannot take a completely constant course, if one looks at larger groups of such economies. With regard to the phenomena of consumption and demand, which are wholly analogous to these, see pp. 82–84.

be extended or modified respectively, in order to include the whole variety of actual economic life; and I have endeavoured to show how the assumption of a completely stationary economy could be replaced by the assumption of a progressive one.

In so far as the new theory of value and capital surpasses all the older theories in profundity and completeness, there can be no doubt that it is destined to play an enlightening part in most of the practical economic controversies of the present time, and to give a valuable indication of the shape of the economic future. I hope very soon to be able to publish some of these applications of the theory.

In conclusion, I express my grateful thanks to the *Lorén Foundation for the Promotion of the Social Sciences*, Stockholm, which has enabled me to publish the present work, and to Herr Otto Gutsche, *wissenschaftlicher Hilfsarbeiter* in the *Statistisches Amt* of Breslau, for the very great care with which he has read the proofs for errors in the language.

THE AUTHOR.

Stockholm, July 1893.

VALUE, CAPITAL AND RENT

Introduction

1—The present-day position of theoretical political economy

At the end of the last century and at the beginning, or during the first third, of the present century the theory of political economy underwent a rapid development—especially in England, at the hands of Adam Smith, Malthus and Ricardo. This seemed to promise that one day this branch of knowledge would be raised to the same level as the exact sciences. Since then, however, this development has not continued on anything like the same scale. As far as interesting works of a special kind on certain branches of political economy—on money and its functions, on banking, on international exchange, etc.—and valuable historical monographs are concerned, modern English literature is not wanting. However, apart from the work of Stanley Jevons, about which we shall have more to say later, no general law worthy to be put beside Malthus's *Law of Population* or Ricardo's *Theory of Rent* has been laid down by any of their followers; for the meritorious work by Cairnes, *Some Leading Principles of Political Economy newly expounded*, contains rather a first step towards, and a stimulus to, renewed and deepened investigation of fundamental economic doctrine than any completed results. J. S. Mill's famous work *Principles of Political Economy*, although already nearly fifty years old, can still—or at least could until quite recently—be regarded as embracing the whole of classical economic knowledge in England.[1]

The same is true of France, whose economic literature, at least during the present century, doubtless includes many eminent writers, but few original thinkers. As far as theoretical political economy is concerned the same applies to German thought, which turned relatively late to the economic sphere, and for a long time was only an echo of the English and French achievements. With the peculiar trend taken by German political economic study in recent times, we shall deal shortly.

In the scientific field not less than in other spheres, however,

[1] Marshall's *Principles of Economics*, which is based throughout on recent investigations, was, when this book was written. not yet published.

stagnation is mostly accompanied by deterioration. When theoretical political economy was no longer able to add new results to those already achieved, the natural consequence was that even the truth of these results was more and more doubted. It was asserted, and not always without reason, that the older economists, in laying down the rules which they regarded as general, only kept in mind the conditions of their own country and their own time. Still more, the question began to be asked whether it was at all possible to work out generally valid laws for a subject which seemed to be influenced in such a high degree by changing circumstances in time, by the peculiar characteristics of different nations, and even by the caprices of human nature itself. This critical, or rather purely negative point of view, which in recent times has also had its advocates in England (Cliff Leslie, J. Ingram and others), has, as is known, become more and more the main line of thought in modern German political economy, where the so-called 'historical school' reigned supreme until quite recently. In the opinion of this school, political economy can only claim to be regarded as a historical subject. Historical inquiries into matters of detail, special investigation of certain limited periods in the development of our continent, as far as transmitted deeds and documents allow—these are the only things which, according to this view, can procure for us a real understanding of economic facts, though necessarily a very fragmentary one. In coming to general conclusions one ought to be extremely cautious; for, *a priori*, it would be quite unrealistic to try to formulate laws, valid for all times and peoples, on the basis of the knowledge which we believe we possess of the general character-istics of human nature and the physical conditions of our life.

In this mode of reasoning there lies, in my opinion, beside a certain amount of truth, a considerable exaggeration. However valuable (indeed even indispensable) historical investigation may be for every social science (and consequently for political economy), it has value only in so far as it succeeds in revealing and throwing light on the general laws which govern and direct human action.[1] Without the existence of such laws,

[1] This was also, if I am not mistaken, the principal aim of the distinguished men who, like Hildebrand, Roscher, Knies and others, inaugurated the historical school in Germany. The one-sidedness which we have mentioned is more the fault of their followers, who, becoming ever more deeply engaged in historical research in special fields, wanted in the end to condemn almost all theory.

history itself would be inconceivable and what it teaches us of no avail to our generation and wholly inapplicable to the conditions of our own time. This is perhaps especially true if we are speaking of those economic relationships which, in their present forms, are to a great extent the product of recent or very recent times, with few or no points of *direct* comparison with the economic life of the past. Let us look at our modern credit and banking system, our system of government finance, industrial associations, international commercial affairs and means of communication. Where would one find, even if one only went back a few centuries, a real counterpart to these at a time when credit banks were unknown, when the guilds enjoyed absolute power, and when trade was so small that, for instance, the whole of the customs business of proud Albion could be leased to private persons for a tribute of a few thousand pounds sterling a year?

That the one-sided, negative course of historical study was especially calculated to raise the influence and prestige of political economy, can scarcely be affirmed. A subject which has not a single established result and no generally acknowledged doctrine to show, must consequently renounce all claim to play a leading part in the decisions and resolutions of governments and parliaments. It was not to be wondered at, then, that in consequence of the purely historical orientation of political economy the opinion should at last have spread to the leading circles that in economic affairs almost everything was possible, and nearly everything permitted, to men who themselves make or wish to make history.[1]

Was it really true that classical political economy, as developed by the above-mentioned great representatives of the

[1] In my opinion, one of the main reasons for this not very satisfactory development of German political economy can without doubt be found in the restriction of the freedom of instruction in this field, especially while the Socialist Law (*Sozialistengesetz*) was in force. Research, when it is forbidden to deal with certain spheres or to draw certain conclusions, does not usually provide us with great results, as experience has shown. The German scholars, naturally enough, preferred to occupy themselves with historical investigations which were relatively innocuous, in order to avoid 'the controversies of the day.' Meanwhile socialism, which it was desired to combat, continued to exist and made more and more disciples, even among scholars. Since its doctrines could no longer be preached openly, they were never subjected to serious criticism. Nowadays, in the writings of German professors, one very often encounters socialist arguments—even those which are least capable of being maintained—in one disguise or another.

subject, was only pretence and delusion? Nobody can affirm
this after having studied carefully the principal works of
Ricardo and Malthus. If the doctrines of political economy
have not so far been able to reform the economy of nations
even partially, the most important reason is simply that these
teachings have never been carried through seriously and to their
full implications. In this case, the great economists had the
same experience as the doctor whose patient sometimes obeyed
his orders and sometimes disobeyed them, but never ceased to
complain of his illness.

That their analysis of economic phenomena was an incomplete one, must be admitted; but this defect need not be
ascribed to the analytic-synthetical method which they applied.
It is to be hoped that this method—continually refined and
developed with the aid of the daily increasing harvest of facts
which are nowadays supplied by statistics and historical
research, as well as by the more profound knowledge which
we now possess of the forces of nature and the economic
resources which they offer—will be able, in theory and in
practice, to bring the doctrines concerning the economic life of
nations, their internal economy and mutual intercourse to an
even higher degree of clarity and harmony.

A promise in this direction is given by the new theory of
exchange value, with conclusions about capital and interest
derived from it, which will be the subject of this study. Already
40 years ago the essential features of this theory were described
in a work—unfortunately totally unnoticed—by the German
H. Gossen.[1] At the beginning of the seventies, it was developed
afresh in an essentially identical form by an Austrian, a French-
Swiss and an English scholar,[2] without one of them being
aware of the work which was being done simultaneously by the
others or of that of their undeservedly forgotten predecessor.

2—The classical theory of value

That the theory of value must be of fundamental significance
for political economy, is evident if one bears in mind that this
subject deals with values only, that is to say with that aspect

---

[1] *Grundsätze des menschlichen Verkehrs und die daraus fliessenden Regeln für
menschliches Handeln*, Brunswick 1853, new edition Berlin 1889.
[2] Carl Menger, Léon Walras, Stanley Jevons.

of external objects (and, in a wider sense, of human abilities and qualities also) which makes it worth while for us to obtain possession of them. In the true natural sciences also, and still more in technology, this point of view is of course of great importance; in political economy, however, it is the only determining one. It is well known that almost every new school of thought in political economy has laid down its own theory of value and from this, as it were, derived its entire character. Here we shall glance briefly at the best known of these theories.

The difficulty in explaining the nature of exchange value as well as in trying to find a suitable measure for it, is a twofold one.

Obviously, objects have a value for us only in virtue of their *utility*, that is to say, because of the enjoyment and satisfaction which they give us, or—and this is fundamentally the same— because of the pain and discomfort from which they free us; but apart from the fact that all these attributes seem, at first glance, on account of their subjective nature, quite unsuited to serve as a real measure of value, we have in addition the peculiar and remarkable fact that 'utility,' however much we may stretch this concept, usually bears no relation to what one calls 'exchange value,' that is to say, the quantitative propor- tions in which the objects are actually exchanged for one another. Adam Smith has indicated this fact in a well-known sentence the paradoxical nature of which does not, however, seem to have been realized either by himself or by his closest adherents: 'The things which have the greatest value in use,' says Adam Smith, 'have frequently little or no value in exchange'; and vice versa—e.g. diamonds, water.

It was noticed by de Quincey and J. S. Mill that, properly speaking, only the first half of Smith's sentence is true. In their opinion the 'value in use' of objects can indeed be greater than their 'value in exchange,' but not vice versa. The value in use would always constitute the upper limit of value in exchange and so forth. In fact, this is only true of the commodity obtained in exchange. The commodity disposed of must, of course, always have (for the owner) a greater value in exchange than in use. The thought indicated here was not, by the way, pursued; rather, it was resolved to leave aside the whole conception of value in use.

Altogether, these subjective grounds of value in exchange

seemed of a nature too indeterminate for the establishment thereon of a science of value. The French school, which, with J. B. Say at the head, tried to adhere to 'utility' as the factor which determines value, became involved thereby in contradictions and difficulties which for a long time were regarded as insurmountable. Only recent investigations, with which we shall deal in the following pages, succeeded in shedding full light on this important but obscure point.

The English school, on the other hand, tried from the start to find another and a more satisfying and objective reason for value in exchange. It believed it had found such a reason in labour. Labour, effort, that price which we must pay for the satisfaction of our needs, where nature herself provides no remedy —labour, this indispensable factor in almost all production, not only seemed to be the most natural explanation of exchange value, but, as a measure of this, also had the important advantage that the length of working hours can be reckoned with the same accuracy as all other physical quantities. In the writings of Adam Smith, who, on the whole, was not a man of exact definitions, this explanation was still rather vague. In Smith's works, labour as a measure of exchange value sometimes means the labour which is necessary for the production of the commodity concerned; at other times—or, rather, in one and the same sentence—he means by it the labour which, once one is in possession of the commodity, one can spare oneself and pass on to others—that is to say, the quantity of labour which the possessor of the commodity concerned is able to 'command' or buy. It is, of course, quite inadmissible, however, to treat these different quantities of labour alike, without going back to primitive conditions of society where interest and rent were unknown. This was most probably what Adam Smith meant but never expressed in clear words. In any case one misses in his works any clear discussion of the significance of interest and rent for the exchange value of commodities.

Ricardo was far from this ambiguity. For him 'labour' is always the quantity of labour required for the production of goods. Nevertheless, he believed he was able to adhere to the dogma that labour is the measure of exchange value. And this dogma he developed with a force and consistency not often found in works on economic questions. The socialists, especially those of the Marxist school, believed, as is well known, that they could use Ricardo's theory of value as a weapon of direct attack against the whole capitalist structure of society. This is certainly wrong.[1] Ricardo's dictum is quite formal. His sole aim was to lay down a general measure and regulator of exchange value; he never speaks of labour as the exclusive source of value, even in our present-day society. On the other hand, the way in which Ricardo develops his argument— totally free from the fantastic ideas and dialectic leaps of many of the later schools—is a model of strictly logical reasoning about a subject which seems, at first glance, to admit of so little precision.

In primitive society where private ownership of land is unknown and where almost no capital exists—for instance, in a society of hunters—labour would, as had already been noticed by Adam Smith, constitute the only source and there-fore also the natural measure of exchange value. If, on the average, it takes three days to kill a beaver but only two days to shoot a stag, two beavers will necessarily be equal to three stags in value. Here already one notices that cause and effect have in reality been confused. For if a beaver's carcass is not valued more highly than a stag's for other reasons, it will certainly never acquire a higher value by the greater difficulty in procuring it. The only consequence would then be that nobody would care to give up his time to work so troublesome and so little remunerative as killing a beaver. Formally speaking, however, this rule is certainly perfectly correct under the given assumptions.

But in our present-day society, where almost all land is private property and almost all production requires capital, can labour be regarded as the only measure of exchange value? Ricardo answers this question in the affirmative, and does so after taking the following points into consideration.

If in the first place no account is taken of rent, or if one looks at those branches of industry which have to pay little rent, the price of their products is divided into two parts, namely wages and capital profits; and though neither of these coincides with the labour employed in their production, according to Ricardo

---

[1] That the Ricardian theory, while exposing the blind and purely mechanical operation of economic forces, must indirectly help the criticism of the order of society, no one, of course, will deny.

they are, nevertheless, each in itself proportional to that quantity of labour, so that finally the reciprocal prices or exchange values of commodities come to stand in the same proportion to each other as the quantities of labour which are necessary for their production.

As regards labour, this is a consequence of the reciprocal competition of workers, whereby wages are always reduced to one and the same level. Here, of course, one must meet the objection that in fact different kinds of labour are generally rewarded very unequally. Ricardo, indeed, has not given sufficient thought to this fact. He simply pointed—as Adam Smith did before him—to the effect of competition, which has apparently been the laying down of a fixed scale of reward for qualified labour which, during longer or shorter periods, remains unchanged. This is not correct, as Cairnes[1] especially has shown in detail: between different grades of workers or of society in general no effective competition exists.

Respecting wages for ordinary labour, Ricardo is known to have laid down the rule that these are not only equal for all workers, but that they can, as far as real wages are concerned, even be regarded as a constant magnitude which, incidentally, is equal to the sum of what the worker himself needs for subsistence and for bringing up the usual number of children. This is the notorious theory of 'natural' wages. Though this theory is not quite true, one can at least say of it that at present it is unfortunately only too true. But we will not proceed further with criticism of this theory here. Later on J. S. Mill (amongst others) substituted for it the so-called wage fund theory, which from the scholarly point of view is even less satisfactory. We shall come back to this later.

The means of subsistence of workers are advanced by capitalists. Capital, if in the meantime one takes no account of the fixed part of it, forms consequently a magnitude which is proportional to the quantity of labour; and, as capital can change its occupation as easily as labour or even more easily, capital profit will be approximately the same, though in different countries or at different times it may change. Ricardo was blamed by several economists for not having examined thoroughly the way in which capital profit came into existence, but simply taking it for granted. I cannot agree with this opinion.

[1] *Some Leading Principles of Political Economy newly expounded.*

The capitalist is for Ricardo the entrepreneur of the firm. Therefore, once he has paid, or rather advanced, wages and rent, he is entitled to the result of the production. Since, according to Ricardo, wages represent a magnitude fixed from the beginning, and since—as he later shows—the level of rent is also determined by independent causes, the cause of capital profit is already settled. It is neither possible nor necessary to explain capital profit in other ways, if the other assumptions are sound.

On the other hand—as Ricardo himself especially emphasizes—his general rule about the proportionality of prices and quantities of labour is considerably modified by the fact that the division of capital into a fixed and working part is not the same in all firms. Only the working part of capital employs and pays wages to workers, whereas the profit is dependent on and proportional to the whole capital. Or, what is in fact the same, each part of the capital employs labour (namely, the labour which is necessary for the construction of machines, etc.) only once during the whole process of production, and until it is replaced by the proceeds of the finished products. But *every* year each part of the capital bears the usual interest or yields the usual profit, until the piece of capital in question is worn out.

The theoretical difficulty presented by this was not solved by Ricardo; and of course it never can be solved in such a way that this proportionality between prices and quantities of labour would still hold good. It should be remembered, however, that here, too, Ricardo has correctly understood the sequence of cause and effect; if money wages rise (which in his view could only happen over longer periods as a result of the greater difficulty in producing the means of maintenance of workers, although in general such a rise can be understood as the consequence of every increase of capital), then the introduction of machines which before proved unproductive will now become more profitable, as he has shown in an ingenious example.[1] The price of machinery, that is to say, includes profit as well as wages. As this profit, like all the others, must fall when wages rise, the price of machines can consequently never rise in the same proportion as wages. According to the more modern terminology, this means that

1 *Principles*, Ch. I, Section V.

every increase of wages encourages a lengthening of the period of production, which occupies more time but is more productive, whereby the wage increase is partly compensated. Indeed, in this example of Ricardo's, the fine theories with which Böhm-Bawerk has recently enriched the subject lie enclosed as in the bud. In these theories the relationships between the rate of interest and wages appear in a strong light, in which, however, they are seen to be less simple than was assumed in Ricardo's 'iron' law of wages or in the wage fund theory.

But apart from labour and means of labour, production also needs natural resources; and in so far as these are not free, but must be bought from the owner of landed property, a new element in the cost of production enters here: rent. If in all production every unit of labour always used exactly the same amount of natural resources (for instance, the same area of land of the same quality), then the reciprocal exchange value of goods would remain proportional to the employed quantity of labour. This, however, is not the case. The different branches of production not only need labour and natural resources in quite unequal proportions, but, even when producing the same kind of goods—as, for example, in agriculture—the same expenditure of labour will yield different quantities of products according to the condition of the land and to the climate.

It is known that the last-mentioned point in particular gave rise to the ingenious theory of rent which bears Ricardo's name, though it really originates from Malthus and Sir Richard West.[1] With growth of population and increasing capital, the demand and prices for agricultural products rise, *ceteris paribus*; this leads to the cultivation of poorer land as well as a more intensive cultivation of land already under the plough. The owners of better land, or the landowners generally, are consequently able to appropriate to themselves as rent from this monopoly a greater and greater share, absolute and relative, of the yield of land. Only the poorest land gives no rent; the last labourer engaged in cultivation only raises products equal in value to his own means of maintenance (including the usual interest, in cases where these were advanced to him by the capitalist). At this extreme point the products of agriculture, in respect of their exchange value, come under the same rules as were valid

---

[1] It is said to have been in fact put forward by a certain Dr. Anderson before Adam Smith, but at that time remained unconsidered.

in actual industry. It is the labour engaged on the poorest land, or, more generally speaking, that agricultural labour which provides no rent, but, nevertheless, does yield profit, that determines, in Ricardo's view, the value of agricultural products. The rule of labour as a measure of value was therefore also applied in this connexion, though, as one finds, in an entirely formal manner. Proportionality of commodity prices with the quantity of labour employed in the production of these goods, is here no longer mentioned.

From this Ricardo drew the familiar conclusion upon which he, and Mill after him, laid great stress, namely that rent constitutes 'no element' of prices of agricultural products; in other words, prices for the latter would not fall, even if the rent were completely remitted by the landowners. This assertion, at first sight paradoxical, certainly contains a profound and remarkable truth; but the truth in it is valid not only for landed property but also for capital in its real sense. According to Ricardo and Mill, if landowners remitted their rent, this would only result in tenants themselves now being able to live 'like gentlemen.' They would then, in fact, become landowners themselves, and would simply put the rent into their own pockets. One could, of course, certainly think of a more generally useful application of rent, e.g. through the nationalization of landed property; or, what is nearly the same, rent could, on the analogy of the net profit of a co-operative society, be distributed *pro rata parte* amongst the consumers of bread. That this would be very advantageous to the latter, is quite evident; for now they could cover part of their consumption of bread by means of these new incomes. But this does not mean that the *price* of bread would fall; on the contrary it would rise; for the consumption and the demand for bread would doubtless increase in these circumstances, while the possibilities of production remained just the same as before.

This rule is also important as opposed to the socialist point of view, according to which all rent is an exploitation of labour which would only receive *its full reward* in the socialist society. However, even in the socialist state, the reward of labour would be substantially the same as now, for it would also depend on the proportion between supply and demand, and could, for instance, never rise above the yield which the last labour employed on the poorest land or in the least fruitful branches of production is able to raise. It is obvious that, if private property were replaced by common property, all who were before without property would get greater incomes; but they would not get these incomes as higher wages for labour, but as a share in the rent of the then nationalized capital (including landed property). In other words, rent and interest are not, as the socialists declare, merely 'historical categories,' but, on the contrary, as Böhm-Bawerk in particular has clearly shown, indestructible economic factors; and this state of affairs, amongst other things, shows the universal significance of the population problem, consideration of which in the socialist state could not be postponed for a single day, let alone for centuries.

Ricardo's theory of value is, one finds, developed with a high degree of consistency and strictness. On the other hand, it is, as we said before, of a purely formal nature; of the inner causes of exchange value this theory gives us practically no explanation. It has, in addition, the fault of choosing two quite different explanations for the prices of commodities in the market and the so-called natural prices. The former are explained as dependent on 'supply and demand'; the latter, however, are explained in the way mentioned above; while nothing seems clearer than that a reason which is sufficient to determine at any given moment the level of prices must be regarded as their only and true cause.

Nevertheless, Ricardo's theory certainly contains a considerable amount of truth. The theory of rent, especially, shows a marked analogy with the modern concept of marginal utility.

A more searching analysis of economic phenomena would certainly have made possible a scientific extension of Ricardo's theory of value. Such an extension, however, was not undertaken; on the contrary, this theory underwent a completely unscientific and paradoxical exaggeration at the hands of two completely opposed schools, the harmony economists (Bastiat among others) on the one hand, and the socialists on the other. The dispassionate and purely scientific investigation of the English scholars had unmercifully exposed the weaknesses of our modern economic life.[1] It now became the task of the

---

[1] There was, in my opinion, a good reason why Ricardo, in showing up these weaknesses, did not treat capital property in the same way as landed property. The former had, at least, the advantage over landed property that its object,

defender of the existing order of society to conceal or explain away these weaknesses as far as possible. It was the aggressors' task, on the contrary, to show them in a particularly strong light. Both trends met strangely in the attempt to establish labour not only as a formal measure of exchange value, but— and from this attempt Ricardo wisely abstained—also as the real cause and substantial ground of value.

3—The theories of value of the harmony economists and the socialists

In Ricardo's system, as we have seen, not only labour, but also capital profit and ground-rent, claimed to get their share of the fruits of production. But are not the latter themselves products of labour? asked Bastiat and his school. Is not capital itself produced by labour, and does not the fertility of the

capital, had first to be created; and the existence of large amounts of capital can only have beneficial consequences for society itself, which could hardly be affirmed of the monopoly of landed property. Adolf Held's reproaches, *Zwei Bücher zur sozialen Geschichte Englands*, are therefore unfounded in my opinion. As to Ricardo's alleged 'harshness' towards the working classes, it should be mentioned that he never represented the low level of wages as the only possible situation for workers, still less as something which is pleasant in itself. How in his opinion workers could achieve a better position at that time, Ricardo has partly shown directly, and partly indicated indirectly, by accepting Malthus's doctrine. As I see it, men like Malthus and Ricardo, who tried to search out the true reason of social conditions and particularly of the low standard of living of workers, have done more for their welfare than those economists who some-times make a great show of friendly feelings towards the workers, but do not want to learn the means which could really have remedied their situation. A German economist, very well known in recent times and very praiseworthy in different ways, has actually delivered an academic speech on the causes of social want without uttering a single word on the population question. In the *Revue d'Economie politique* of November 1891, the same author made the astonishing statement that Karl Marx has 'refuté la thèse, en conséquence de laquelle le salaire devait dépendre de l'augmentation ou de la diminution de la population totale, au lieu de dépendre de l'excès existant *dans chaque industrie*, et cela de telle manière qu'elle ne devrait plus être soutenue dans les cercles scientifiques.' Probably as a proof of this alleged victory of Marx over Ricardo and Malthus, it is later mentioned that the attempts of the coal-miners of Durham and Northumberland to improve their situation during the prosperous period that followed the Franco-Prussian war, failed because new workers from other branches of industry came from all parts of the United Kingdom. 'Ce fut surtout des matelots qui s'y rendirent.'

For ordinary readers, this example will speak *against* Marx's view and in favour of Ricardo's. How the author could have overlooked this, is beyond my understanding.

cultivated land depend on the labour of former generations? They answered both these questions in the affirmative, and believed they had achieved by this a considerable improvement on Ricardo's theory. All value became now an indirect or direct product of labour; not only the true capitalist but also the owner of landed property obtained as his profit only the reward of his own and his ancestors' labour, or the reward of his renunciation in not having consumed the fruits of this labour. It needs few words to show how absurd this view is, especially as regards landed property. Let us look merely at the extreme cases. What human hand ever gave value to our forests, coal-fields, ore-seams, natural meadows and pastures, fish-ponds, etc.; what human hand 'created' the source of returns which they give to their owners? The matter does not wear a much better aspect if one tries to explain these unproduced values as the fruits of the industrial labour of the whole society, as Leroy-Beaulieu did in his work *Répartition des Richesses*. This is a point which, as is well known, Lasalle also tried to make, but in the socialist interest. A vacant building site in the middle of a well populated town has, as everybody knows, a very high value. Is this value also a product of the local industries? This is certainly a confusion of ideas. The real cause of this phenomenon is not the productivity of industry or labour, but the fact that this labour is not sufficiently productive. In spite of all hard work, all improvements of the means of communication, etc., a numerous town population cannot overcome the inconveniences which are caused by increasing distances. This is the cause of the high value of central building sites or open spaces. What is *given* for them may indeed be the creation of industry, but not their value itself, which, on the contrary, is determined by the sum of the needs which they satisfy. There can, of course, be cases where human thought or hand can sometimes give a high value to things which were hitherto worthless, without any direct influence. It is said, for instance, that, through the introduction of the Bessemer method in the iron-industry, certain ores[1] which in former times were thought valueless have proved to be the best material for the new process, so that the owners of the ore-seams in question suddenly found themselves in possession of considerable wealth. Up to a certain point one

[1] If I am not wrong, the so-called specular iron-ore.

can, of course, regard this value as a product of Bessemer's inventive genius, but it would be quite absurd to try to find any *proportion* between the labour which in this case Bessemer employed for his invention (even if the labour of all his predecessors were included) and the values, perhaps quite unknown to him, which they later produced or, rather, revealed. Even Leroy-Beaulieu does not go so far.

If the attempt of the harmony economists to explain all value as a product of labour failed in this way, even as a scientific theory, this was even more the case when they tried to make the question of the exchange value of commodities into a question of the justification of the distribution of wealth in society. In this theory, indeed, they believed they had indicated a new and better legal argument for the existing distribution of property. Questions of social justice turn out in the end to be questions of what is socially useful and possible; and no one, however learned or sagacious he may be, can claim for the majority of the present possessors of capital and rent a right higher than that which lies in the instinct of self-preservation—I mean the right of self-defence, which, by the way, is not wholly objectionable.

The rule: He who tries to prove too much, proves nothing, has seldom been better exemplified than in this case. The writings of the harmony economists became indeed the arsenal from which their opponents, the socialists, took their sharpest weapons of attack against the existing order of society. It is known to what merciless satire Bastiat and his German follower Schulze-Delitzsch—on the whole an excellent economist—were exposed by Lasalle. The socialists agreed only too willingly with the doctrine of their opponents, that labour is the only source of value. But as soon as it became necessary to answer the question, who was at present actually performing, or in bygone days had actually performed, that labour, the socialists thought—and not without reason—that the credit must necessarily be awarded to those classes which one usually calls the working classes.

This is not the place to go into a more detailed analysis of the socialist doctrines, which in fact include many things which do not stand or fall by this or that economic theory. But in their criticism of the present system of production as well as in the estimate of economic resources which they themselves recommend, the socialist authors are to a great extent under the influence of the peculiar theory of value which, since the first writings of Marx, has become more and more the pillar of the socialist system. The so-called proof which Marx gives of his rule that labour is the substance of exchange value, whilst unpaid labour equals the profit of capitalists, on which his extensive work *Das Kapital* is only a continuous commentary, has, in fact, as is now most probably more and more admitted, scarcely the virtue of being able to be discussed seriously. It consists of a kind of free application of the *principium exclusi tertii*. If two commodities are exchanged against each other in the market, they must, says Marx, be equal in some one respect. But the equality cannot consist in the fact that they have the same value in use; on the contrary, this must necessarily be different, otherwise the exchange would be senseless. The values in use of different commodities are indeed incommensurable[1] quantities (says Marx), and nothing is consequently left but that both commodities are the product of an equally long working time. Or, as the same thought is expressed by Marx elsewhere: If one divests commodities of the specific attributes which determine their values in use (which cannot be compared with one another), there is only one attribute left, namely that of being 'labour jelly' (*Arbeitsgallerte*), definite masses of 'congealed labour time.' The gaping holes in this argument hardly require special mention. Even if the values in use of two different commodities, or the utility which they have at any time, were quite incomparable magnitudes and could consequently not be taken into consideration, there could generally exist a great number of circumstances besides labour which together could, without being the same for both commodities, constitute the same exchange value. For instance, both have used a certain area of land for the production of raw material as well as for the production of the finished commodity; for both of them a certain quantity of power (coal) was needed to bring them to market, etc. But as regards working time, not only its length, but also the intervals between different stages of production, in other words the time during which the means of maintenance

---

[1] This expression occurs only here and there in Marx's work—e.g. on page 96, n. 80, of the third edition of *Das Kapital*—but it expresses exactly his true meaning.

and of production for the workers must be advanced, have influence on the productivity of labour.[1]

In reality, however, the different values in use or the 'utilities' are by *no means incommensurable quantities*. Every day we compare different utilities with one another and weigh their reciprocal magnitudes against each other. If, following the Marxist terminology, we divest two commodities of their specific attributes, one attribute will always remain: both commodities provide us with a certain quantity of utility. But this utility does *not* need to be equal for both commodities, for them to possess the same exchange value. The fixed proportions in which different goods are exchanged against each other in the open market, are indeed the consequence of special laws which are valid *for the market* but not for the individual exchange—in the first place, the *la wof free competition*, or the *law of indifference* as Jevons called it, according to which at every moment and for every commodity there can be approximately only *one* price on the market.

In what follows we shall have an opportunity to go deeper into most of the above-mentioned points of view, which together form the framework of the modern theory of exchange value. The considerations which have led to the formulation of this

[1] If working time alone determined exchange value, it would make no difference to the value or to the quantity of the product whether, for example, 10 workers took 10 years to produce it or 100 workers a single year. This, in fact, cannot be true, because otherwise it would never be profitable to invest capital in the longer period of production.

How it was that Marx could simply deny all these indisputable and well-known facts, and what he meant when, for example, he assures us that virgin soil, natural meadows, wild-growing wood, etc., are 'values in use, but not values' (*Das Kapital*, vol. I, third edition, page 7), etc. etc., is indeed not easy to understand. In the first volume of *Das Kapital* these contradictions are as far as possible covered by the general assertion, never elucidated, that prices (even average prices) must not be treated simply as if they were identical with values. On page 202, n. 31, the promise is given that this secret will be disclosed in the third, not yet published volume. The necessary explanation will in any case come rather late!

Meanwhile one can confidently assert that the solution of this puzzle lies simply in the fact that Marx, like Rodbertus before him, does *not* mean by value the *real* exchange value, but rather certain ideal exchange values which would come into being as soon as capital and landed property ceased to be private property.

Even if we assume this, the rule that labour is the only substance of exchange value is, as we have already seen, by no means correct; but then it would represent at least a possible and comprehensible point of view, which can scarcely be affirmed of the present Marxist theory of value, if one takes it literally.

theory are, however, not of a kind that can be easily understood, and one cannot reproach Marx with not having thought of them. Less excusable, it seems to me, is the fact that modern socialist writers—for example, B. K. Kautsky in his well-known account of Marx's fundamental doctrines—show themselves totally uninfluenced by recent investigations, although these investigations have attracted increasingly lively interest in the learned world.

This brief survey of the history of the development of different theories of value will have sufficed to show two things: firstly, that the question of the origin of exchange value, far from being a more or less unfruitful splitting of hairs, is on the contrary of the most far-reaching practical interest; secondly, that the heart of the matter lay so deep down that, to find it, a new and more profound investigation was indeed necessary. Such an investigation was in fact carried out in recent times— in England, by the highly gifted Stanley Jevons, who died too early; in Switzerland, by Léon Walras, professor at the Academy of Lausanne; and also in Austria, where Carl Menger and his disciples—amongst whom Böhm-Bawerk must be mentioned first—have devoted themselves with as much zeal as good fortune to these investigations.

I
The New Theory of Value

1—The concept of value according to Jevons, Walras and the Austrian school

An account of the recent theory of value can suitably begin with a revision of Adam Smith's rule already mentioned—the rule that the value in use and the exchange value are independent of one another. With de Quincey and Mill, we have seen that such a complete independence does not exist; on the contrary the value in use—understood as the benefit or enjoyment which a person thinks he has or expects to gain from an object—must necessarily be greater in the case of the object taken in exchange than in the case of the object given in exchange, and this for *each* of the exchanging persons. In the last-mentioned statement of fact an important state of affairs is already expressed; for it follows from this with mathematical necessity that the objects which are about to be exchanged for one another must stand, in respect of their value in use for one of the parties to the exchange, in a sequence opposite to that in which they stand for the other. In other words, the value in use of an object is no constant magnitude, but changes with different persons and under different circumstances; *and this attribute of value in use is a necessary condition of exchange and consequently of exchange value.* Not to have considered this, is a fundamental defect of Smith's reasoning. The value in use is for him, as can easily be seen, the average utility, or perhaps even the greatest possible utility which an object or a certain quantity of goods of the same kind can possibly have. This utility does not, however, determine the exchange value; the latter is on the contrary regulated by what Jevons calls *final utility* and Wieser *marginal utility*: by the *smallest* utility which an object or the quantity of goods concerned really possesses or presumably will possess.[1]

This matter becomes especially simple if one thinks of the very unequal degree of utility which any quantity of consumer

[1] The ratio of exchange of two objects will consequently depend, even in the case of the simple exchange, on at least *four* factors, namely on the marginal utility of each object for each of the exchanging persons.

goods can possess for us and of the unequal value which we are therefore accustomed to ascribe to them, according to whether we are already provided for a certain period of consumption with a greater or smaller supply of the article in question. Let us consider an example which Böhm-Bawerk gives of a colonist living alone in the virgin forest, whose entire wealth consists of a supply of corn which he has just harvested and which must suffice until the next harvest. One sack of corn will be absolutely necessary to him if he is to maintain life during the winter; another sack gives him enough nourishment to preserve his health and bodily strength; a third sack would be superfluous, but is nevertheless valuable because it enables him to keep poultry, and thus procures for him a desired change in an otherwise purely cereal diet; a fourth sack he converts into spirits. If, finally, he possesses in addition to that a fifth sack, he can procure for himself in exchange for it no greater increase of his well-being than, for example, the amusement of feeding parrots.

If we now suppose that our Robinson Crusoe is offered some other commodity in exchange for one of his sacks of corn, then it is clear that the value (according to his estimate) of the quantity of corn which he would dispose of, would be wholly determined by the least urgent of the above-mentioned modes of application, or by the need to which it corresponds. The sack he disposes of will not be one of the first four, but only the fifth; in other words, if he thinks the utility of the commodity offered him high enough to compensate him for the amusement of keeping parrots, he on his part will be prepared to make the exchange. If, however, he is asked afterwards to part with a further sack of corn and consequently to give up the enjoyment of spirits, which the possession of this sack had made possible for him, the object which is offered him now must be considerably more tempting than would be necessary in the previous case; and of course far more tempting still, if he is to be induced to exchange the third sack also, after which he would not be able to procure for himself animal food. Since the last two sacks are of fundamental importance for his life and health, he will not be able to make up his mind to exchange these even under the strongest temptation.[1]

---

[1] Strictly speaking, however, a decreasing utility will have to be distinguished also *within* the different modes of application of the supply of corn. The marginal

From this very nicely chosen example one learns at the same time, at least in its general features, the role which scarcity on the one hand and costs of production on the other—the two sources from which, according to the older theory, the natural value alternatively arises—really play in determining exchange value. Scarcity itself cannot, of course, increase the utility which the commodities in question are able to provide; but scarcity does, indirectly, ensure that, amongst the needs which can be satisfied at all by a certain kind of goods, only the most urgent ones will in fact be covered, so that even the least among them, which becomes the determining one for the exchange value, will still have a high significance. If our colonist had harvested instead of five sacks only three, the exchange of a single sack would already have deprived him of the possibility of procuring for himself animal food, etc.

As regards cost of production, one sees immediately that the colonist's valuation of the different sacks by no means rises or falls with the expenditure of labour or with the effort which production of these has cost him. More probably, the opposite is the case. If he had been content with the production of only one or two sacks of corn, he could, perhaps, have achieved this by a working-time of merely one or two hours daily, and an effort so moderate would probably have given him more enjoyment than trouble. With each lengthening of working-time the laboriousness of labour increases, while the utility of the product, even if for every new amount of labour it is quantitatively the same, becomes smaller and smaller. When finally the toil becomes so great and the value of the probable product so small that, according to the estimate of the colonist, they approximately counterbalance each other, labour must logically cease.

We can, therefore, not speak positively of an intrinsic, value-creating power in labour. Labour, labour-time, or energy of labour is, on the contrary, to be understood as a commodity like every other, the subjective estimation of which, if it is still in the possession of the worker himself, depends on how much of it he has already disposed of or, according to the established order of labour, will dispose of, and how much he

utility of corn for the colonist will therefore finally be *the same* in *all* modes of application, however different their importance for his welfare may be. Compare the following section.

has consequently left for himself for sleeping, meals, family life, recreation purposes, etc. Every process of production, whether carried on with capital or without, can, resolved into its elements, always be understood as a kind of exchange, whose only fundamental condition is that, like every exchange, it must bring a *gain of utility* (*Nutzgewinn*) to both sides.

This, however, does not prevent the proportionality between exchange value and employed quantity of labour or other costs of production from holding good within certain limits, but it does so only as a *secondary law* (Böhm-Bawerk), since, in the case of free competition, capital, labour and natural resources are always attracted to the most remunerative branches of production until, through an increased supply (diminished scarcity) of the goods concerned, their exchange value decreases, and at the same time the conditions under which they are produced usually become more difficult, so that finally this branch of production becomes no more remunerative than the others.

All the facts mentioned here are, as will be admitted, of the simplest and most obvious kind, and it can scarcely be supposed that they could have been unknown to the great thinkers who have occupied themselves with economic problems. The novelty lies in the idea of establishing the variability of the value in use or of the subjective estimate of value—that small thing, so easily overlooked—as the sole principle of the whole theory of exchange value.

Once found, this principle is seen to be not only sufficiently general to include all the phenomena of exchange, but also so exact that full mathematical precision and sharpness can be given to it, and through it to the whole theory of exchange.

Let us first of all take the simplest case—from which the more complicated one can later be derived—that a certain commodity is not available (for the period concerned) by direct production, that it cannot be replaced by another kind of goods, and finally, that it can be divided in any way one pleases and consumed in any quantities. According to what we said before, it is clear that the utility of a new unit of quantity of this commodity can be regarded as a *function* in the mathematical sense—a decreasing function—of the quantity of the possessed supply as the (sole) variable. If, furthermore, one thinks of this supply as successively diminished, every unit of quantity to be omitted represents a new, different utility, and the sum of these utilities can be nothing else but the total utility of the supply in question. The marginal utility appears, therefore, as the *differential coefficient* of the total utility, as its first derivative with respect to the possessed quantity of goods as variable.

It is seldom a question of measuring this total utility itself. This can sometimes even be regarded as infinite or immeasurably great; usually only smaller changes of the supply or of the usual quantities of consumption of a commodity are concerned. However, the marginal utility is only measured in so far as it is compared with the marginal utility of other goods or of the same commodity under changed circumstances. But the possibility of doing this, in other words, the notion of values in use of *different* goods as commensurable, not incommensurable, is a postulate of the modern theory of value. As we shall see, the principle of thrift demands in the case of the simple exchange of goods which can be divided in any way, that exchange is carried out up to the point at which the small quantities of goods which are the last to be exchanged have the same utility—for each of the exchanging persons. If the commodities on both sides are measured according to conventional units of quantities, then this may also be expressed as follows: after having settled the exchange, the marginal utilities on both sides must stand in the same proportion as their respective prices. In the end, therefore, it may be possible to alter Smith's rule already mentioned in such a way, perhaps, as to say that the exchange value of goods is really proportional to their value in use, namely to the value in use, or the utility, *of the last unit of quantity of the commodity in question, given or taken in exchange.*

Moreover, as we have already indicated above, ratios of exchange, real *values* of exchange, occur only under the influence of the market, and there also only approximately.

In the case of the individual exchange, both contracting parties can in general still find their profit in the exchange within rather wide limits; *what* the price will be within these bounds—in other words, in what proportions the goods in question will at last be exchanged against each other—depends on a great many circumstances: on the power of judgment, habits, and equanimity of each of the contracting parties, on the fair-mindedness of both, etc. Only in the open market, where most of these individual attributes and considerations are neutralized by universal competition, as we know from experience, there will be approximately only one price for every commodity, as is in fact assumed by the theory.

In this chapter as well as in the following one, I shall avail myself rather extensively of the method introduced by Jevons and Walras, which uses mathematical signs and symbols. Although this method is becoming increasingly common in economic literature, it will perhaps be appropriate to say a few words in justification thereof. The older attempts (by Canard amongst others) at a mathematical mode of treatment are said not to have been very happy. For the majority of economists it was, for a long time at any rate, a settled question that greater exactitude in the modes of reasoning and an extension of our knowledge cannot be gained in this way. Stuart Mill (in his *Logic*) also expresses the same thought. He reminds us of the fact that even in one of the highly mathematical sciences, astronomy, a problem so simple at first sight as that of the mutual attraction, and the movement caused thereby, of three celestial bodies (the famous three-body-problem), has so far defied all attempts at an exact mathematical treatment. All the more, he argues, must this be so in the case of the infinitely more complicated economic phenomena.

However, the example chosen would only have been convincing if Mill had shown that, whilst a mathematical treatment of the three-body-problem has never been attempted with success—this, by the way, is only true of the general aspect of this problem—some *other* mode of treatment of the problem might be attempted with more success. This would obviously be absurd. But the same is probably true of every science that deals with measurable quantities, whose mutual relations it tries to investigate. In so far as it does this, it *is* undoubtedly a mathematical subject. If the subject cannot be treated to some extent in a mathematical way, it cannot be treated at all: it contains at best a description of the phenomena in question, but it can never throw light upon their inner relationship.

It is another question, of course, whether we shall be able to pursue economic events and their laws so far that the use of mathematical formulae, equations, etc., will prove really useful —that is to say, really help to clarify and sharpen the reasoning. In this respect, I think, the works of Walras and Jevons can speak for themselves. In particular, I should like to draw attention to the equations which, in the problem of exchange of three (or several) commodities, express the quantities of goods exchanged and their prices. Without the help of mathematical symbols it would not be easy to express or derive these relationships with sufficient precision. It is also worth mentioning that the economists of the Austrian school, which avoids the use of mathematical symbols on principle, have not touched upon this problem at all, although it is fundamental for the whole theory of exchange (in so far as its discussion brings out clearly the significance of trade as well as of money).

I hope, too, that the mathematical dress in which, in the second chapter, I shall clothe Böhm-Bawerk's theory of the relationship between capital interest and wages, will be found to give greater simplicity and clarity to this fine theory; just as the completion of this theory, which I myself first put forward,[1] and which also takes into consideration rent, could scarcely be given in any other form than a mathematical one.

One must, of course, beware of expecting from this method more than it can give. Out of the crucible of calculation[2] comes not an atom more truth than was put in. The assumptions being hypothetical, the results obviously cannot claim more than a very limited validity. The mathematical expression ought to facilitate the argument, clarify the results, and so guard against possible faults of reasoning—that is all.

It is, by the way, evident that the *economic* aspects must be the determining ones everywhere: economic truth must never be sacrificed to the desire for mathematical elegance. In my opinion, neither Jevons nor Walras has transgressed this rule, but their German follower Launhardt has done so several times.

2—Different uses of the same kind of commodity

The simplest form of exchange is that in which the owner of a quantity of goods can and will make different uses of its different parts. The above-mentioned colonist, for example, will keep for himself, his poultry and parrots only a part of his stock of corn for food purposes; the rest he will convert into spirits. It is obvious, then, that he must proportion the

---

[1] An extract from this part of my work was published in *Conrads Jahrbücher*, December 1893.

[2] A true method of calculating will probably not be arrived at for a long time.

two parts to each other in such a way that the marginal utility on both sides becomes the same—in such a way, that is to say, that the last quantity of the remaining corn gives him the same enjoyment as the last quantity of the corn converted into spirits.

Put into an analytical form, this would be expressed as follows: The smallest enjoyment of one unit—for example, one kilogram of corn (the marginal utility of corn)—is conceived as a diminishing function of the supply which still remains after converting part of it into spirits. If, for example, the original supply consisted of a kilograms of corn, and x kilograms of it have already been converted into spirits, so that $a - x$ kilograms of corn are left, the marginal utility of corn, which was originally $F(a)$, has now *risen* to $F(a - x)$. In the same way the smallest enjoyment of one kilogram of corn converted into spirits (marginal utility of spirits or, more properly, of corn used for making spirits) is a diminishing function of the quantity of corn used in this way, and can consequently be expressed by $f(x)$. Then the solution of this problem consists simply of equating these two functional values:

$$F(a - x) = f(x) \qquad (1)$$

Or one could conceive the marginal utility of spirits directly as a function of the quantity of spirits produced. If we suppose that from m kilograms of corn one obtains one litre of spirits, the supply of spirits produced amounts to $\frac{x}{m}$ litres. The enjoyment of the last litre of spirits produced must then be expressed by $f_1\left(\frac{x}{m}\right)$, where f_1 represents a new function. But now, when equilibrium has occurred, this enjoyment must be as great as the enjoyment of the last m units of the remaining corn, or, which is the same, the marginal utility of spirits (enjoyment of one litre of spirits) must be m-times as great as the marginal utility of corn (enjoyment of one kilogram of corn).[1] We therefore write

$$m \cdot F(a - x) = f_1\left(\frac{x}{m}\right)$$

and the problem would be solved—if one knew the forms of the functions $F(\ )$ and $f(\ )$ or $f_1(\ )$, and could replace them by

[1] It is, of course, assumed that for very small changes the marginal utility is approximately constant.

exact mathematical expressions. Then it would only remain to solve the first or the second of the above equations for x, which would be a purely mathematical task. Our colonist solves the same problem by the experimental method, without having heard anything of this theory. When he has produced too little spirits, he distils some more; if he has produced too much, so that the remaining supply of corn is insufficient for his purposes, he will take particular note of this experience for the next year.

But even without knowing the exact forms of the functions, from these equations one can draw an important conclusion, which can, of course, also be easily arrived at without using any symbols. For one could also conceive the *whole* utility or value in use of the remaining supply of corn or of the quantity of corn converted into spirit as functions of the quantities in question—functions which, of course, *grow* with the variable quantities, but more slowly than these. If we express them by $\phi(a - x)$ and $\psi(x)$, the marginal utilities $F(a - x)$ and $f(x)$ are, as we have already shown, their differential coefficients, the former with respect to $(a - x)$, the latter with respect to x.

If one sets oneself the task of determining x in such a way that

$$\phi(a - x) + \psi(x)$$

becomes a maximum, this problem can, as is known, be solved by making the differential coefficient of the sum with respect to x equal to zero. One consequently has

$$\frac{d}{dx}\phi(a - x) + \frac{d}{dx}\psi(x) = 0$$

or, since

$$\frac{d}{dx}\phi(a - x) = -\frac{d}{d(a - x)}\phi(a - x) = -F(a - x)$$

and

$$\frac{d}{dx}\psi(x) = f(x)$$

$$F(a - x) = f(x)$$

which is the same equation as the one found at the beginning.

In other words, the solution of our original problem forms at the same time the solution of the problem of distributing the supply of corn between its two uses in such a way that the greatest possible total utility or total enjoyment arises from it.

This, however, is self-evident; for the purpose of the production of spirits was just to obtain from one part of the supply of corn a higher enjoyment than was obtainable by its direct consumption; and the production will be continued as long as a further gain of utility is obtainable, that is to say, until the greatest possible utility is attained.

Beyond this, almost nothing, as was said before, is known *a priori* about the behaviour of the functions $\phi(\ )$ and $\psi(\ )$ or $F(\ )$ and $f(\ )$. At the outset it is only certain that $\phi(\ )$ and $\psi(\ )$ grow with the variable quantities under the sign of the function, but more slowly than these, and when these disappear, they become zero themselves. From this it follows that their differential quotients $F(\ )$ and $f(\ )$ are *diminishing* functions. The *simplest* approximating formula which satisfies these conditions is the one in which z indicates any variable quantity:

$$\phi(z) = \alpha z - \beta z^2, \quad \psi(z) = \alpha' z - \beta' z^2$$

consequently

$$F(z) = \alpha - 2\beta z, \quad f(z) = \alpha' - 2\beta' z$$

where α and β, α' and β' respectively are positive constants, whose values must be determined for each case. If here, for example, β is very small compared with α, then at first $\phi(z)$ increases almost proportionally with z, but afterwards more and more slowly, reaching a maximum for $z = \frac{1}{2}\frac{\alpha}{\beta}$; after that it decreases, finally becoming zero and even negative. The same is true of $\psi(z)$, if one replaces α and β by α' and β' respectively.

$F(z)$ and $f(z)$, on the contrary, have for small values of z almost the constant values α and α'; if z increases, they always decrease; they become zero where $z = \frac{1}{2}\frac{\alpha}{\beta}$ and $z = \frac{1}{2}\frac{\alpha'}{\beta'}$ respectively; and beyond that they become negative.

In this there is nothing which is inconsistent with experience, for the total utility as well as the marginal utility of a quantity of goods can finally become 'negative,' that is to say, can change into *disutility*, if the existing quantity becomes much too great. For example: water, manure, dross, sawdust, etc.

But what it does not show is whether so simple an approximating formula meets even one single case sufficiently *exactly* to be applicable. In most cases, this is even most improbable. Launhardt, however, has made the most extensive use in his work[1] of precisely this formula, without really examining even once how far it corresponds to the facts. It is at least doubtful, therefore, whether the fine results and conclusions which, by the help of this approximating formula, he has found and printed in italics, have anything to do with reality.

Nevertheless, it will be possible to assert, according to the analogy of physical events, that, if it is only a question of variations *within certain narrower limits*, such an approximating formula can be substituted *within this sphere* for the exact form of the functions, whatever the nature of the latter may otherwise be.

If, for instance, in our example above it is quite certain in advance that the value of x sought[2] must lie between two limits b and c, which are known to lie not too far apart, it will be possible *within these limits* to use without hesitation the approximating formulae; that is to say, instead of equation (1)

$$F(a - x) = f(x)$$

we write

$$\alpha - 2\beta(a - x) = \alpha' - 2\beta' x$$

In order to be able in this case to determine the constants α, β, α', β', it is necessary to know for at least two values of x which belong to this sphere, the corresponding four values of the functions of the marginal utilities $F(a - x)$ and $f(x)$.[3] If we suppose that for $x = b$ the marginal utility of corn is v and the marginal utility of the corn converted into spirits v', and that for $x = c$ their values are w and w' respectively, α, β, α', β' can easily be expressed by v, w, v' and w', and we obtain

$$x = \frac{(v - v')(a - c) - (w - w')(a - b)}{v - v' - (w - w')}$$

or

$$= a - \frac{c(v - v') - b(w - w')}{v - v' - (w - w')}$$

This expression is, as can be seen, homogeneous in relation to the

[1] *Mathematische Begründung der Volkswirtschaftslehre*, Leipzig 1885.

[2] The use of the word 'value' in a *mathematical* sense, that is to say, simply as synonymous with 'magnitude,' which occurs here and quite often in what follows, will, I hope, give no occasion for misunderstanding.

[3] Properly speaking, one therefore needs only to know the three ratios of these four values, as we shall see.

magnitude of v, v', w and w' and of degree zero. In other words, the value of x remains unchanged, irrespective of the measure according to which the marginal utility is estimated; only for *both* kinds of commodities or uses in question this measure must be one and the same. This, of course, cannot be otherwise. The utility of a commodity is something *sui generis*; it can be measured neither in metres nor in kilograms; it is comparable only with itself or with the utility of other goods.

The understanding of the whole matter is greatly facilitated if one conceives it geometrically according to the method employed by Gossen, Jevons and others. The successively diminished supply of corn and the marginal utilities belonging to it, both measured according to an optional unit, can be represented as abscissa and ordinate of a curve, whose area[1] represents the total utility according to the principles of the integral calculus. In the same way the marginal utility of the quantity of corn converted into spirits can be expressed by the ordinate of another curve whose abscissa, which represents this quantity itself, is measured *from point a towards the left.*

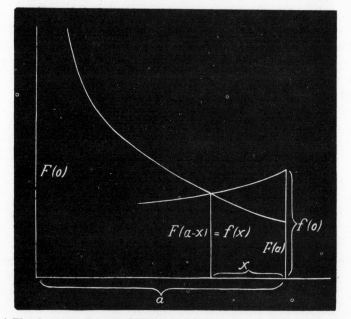

[1] That is to say, the area which is bounded by the curve, both the axes of co-ordinates, and the ordinate in question.

The solution of this problem now consists simply in finding the point of intersection of these two curves. The use of the approximating formula simply tells us that both curves can be regarded as *straight lines* near the point of intersection (as is usual, if it is a question of short pieces).

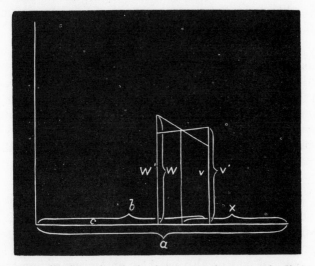

The rest will then simply be interpreted geometrically.

3—Exchange at given prices

If we now turn to exchange in its real sense, we can first deal with the simple case, where the proportion of exchange of two commodities—or, if we conceive one of them as the price commodity[1] and the other as the commodity, the *price* of the latter—is already fixed in advance, as, for example, is approximately the case in the retail trade. The buyer of the commodity then provides himself with so much of it and disposes of so much of the price commodity—in a proportion of exchange which has been fixed by the seller—so that finally the proportion of the marginal utilities of both commodities for the intended consumption period just equals the price.

Let us suppose, for example, that he has at the beginning the quantity *b* of the price commodity, or *b* units, but is still without the commodity, and that he must give for one unit of

[1] That is, the commodity in terms of which price will be expressed. (Translator's note.)

the commodity p units of the price commodity. If we then express the marginal utility of the commodity by $F(\ )$ and the marginal utility of the price commodity by $f(\ )$, we get

$$F(x) = p \cdot f(b - y)$$

where x indicates the number of the acquired units of the commodity and y the number of units of the price commodity given in exchange. Moreover, we have here

$$y = p \cdot x$$

so that the problem is solved as soon as the forms of the functions $F(\ )$ and $f(\ )$ are known. Very often it will happen that the function $f(\ )$ is a constant. If, for example, the price commodity is money, its marginal utility is determined by the income or even by the total wealth of the buyer, and these magnitudes do not as a rule vary noticeably by a single exchange. We have then quite simply

$$F(x) = p \cdot v$$

if by v we express the constant utility of the unit of money (for the buyer), or what is usually called the 'value of one £' or of 'one florin,' and if the price of one unit of the desired commodity amounts to p£ or florins at the moment. Within suitable limits, one could, of course, also use here an approximating formula of the first degree for $F(\ )$ [and $f(\ )$]; for instance, when x lies near a,

$$F(x) = p_1 \cdot v + w\frac{a - x}{c}$$

after which

$$F(x) = p \cdot v$$

becomes

$$x = a + c \cdot \frac{v}{w} \cdot (p_1 - p)$$

p_1 expresses here the *average* price of the commodity, a the quantity of it which the buyer in question *usually* buys; w and c are two constants, which, for the sake of symmetry, we have chosen in such a way that w shall express a magnitude of value or utility, and c a quantity of goods. The last equation, then, tells us that if the price demanded is a little under or over the average price, the buyer in question will purchase and consume more or less than usual of the commodity for the consumption period concerned *in proportion to the difference of price*.

That the price on the part of the seller is unalterably fixed, supposes, of course, that for him neither the marginal utility of the commodity nor that of the price commodity is altered by the exchange. This can happen either through the fact that his supply of the commodity concerned is very large in comparison with the quantity to be exchanged, or through the fact that he himself is only the connecting link between the real barterers, as in the wholesale trade. How in the last case the price is in fact determined, is a problem in itself, which we cannot deal with for a long time yet. It is clear, of course, that here also a maximum problem is solved. Suppose that for the buyer the total utility of the quantity of goods is expressed by $\phi(x)$ and the total utility of the price commodity by $\psi(b - y)$. If he now wants to gain the greatest possible utility, that is to say, if $\phi(x) + \psi(b - y)$ is to be a maximum, we must get

$$\frac{d}{dx}\phi(x)dx + \frac{d}{dy}\psi(b - y)dy = 0$$

But according to what has gone before,

$$\frac{d}{dx}\phi(x) = F(x)$$

and

$$\frac{d}{dy}\psi(b - y) = -\frac{d}{d(b - y)}\psi(b - y) = -f(b - y)$$

We therefore obtain

$$F(x)dx = f(b - y)dy$$

dx and dy express here the small quantities of goods last exchanged against each other. Their proportion is consequently the constant price p. Or, which is the same, from the equation $y = p \cdot x$ we obtain $dy = pdx$. We have consequently

$$F(x) = p \cdot f(b - y)$$

as above.

4—Isolated exchange

If for *both* the exchanging persons the marginal utility of one or other of the commodities in question, which we will call (A) and (B), is altered by the exchange, and consequently the price is not fixed in advance, then—supposing the exchange to be completely isolated, that is to say, supposing that other possibilities of obtaining the desired commodity do not exist—

one cannot possibly speak of a fixed proportion of exchange which can be theoretically determined: the problem is *indeterminate*. Only this much is certain, that an exchange will take place wherever both contracting parties derive, or believe that they derive, advantage from it, and that it will continue as long as it promises a further gain of utility on both sides, be it ever so small. If we suppose in particular, as we also did in the previous cases, that it is a matter of continuous quantities, that is to say, of commodities which are optionally divisible and can also be consumed in optional quantities, it can be asserted that the exchange will cease only at the point at which the proportion of the marginal utility of the one commodity to that of the other is equal *on both sides*. If this condition is not yet fulfilled there will always exist on *both* sides a reason for continuing the exchange. If, after the exchange has taken place, in the estimation of the original possessor of (*A*) one unit of the commodity (*B*) is still equal in value to three units of the commodity (*A*), whilst the possessor of (*B*) estimates that this quantity is equal to only $2\frac{1}{2}$ units of the commodity (*A*), then both believe that they will obtain an increase if the second of the contracting parties gives to the former another or several units of the commodity (*B*) against, for example, $2\frac{3}{4}$ units each of the commodity (*A*). But this tells us neither in what proportion the previous exchange took place nor how great the quantities were, nor consequently in what average proportion both commodities finally change their possessors.

The mathematical manner of treatment reflects this fact clearly. Let us suppose that one possessor has *a* units of the commodity (*A*), but as yet no units of (*B*); and that the other possessor has no units of (*A*), but *b* units of (*B*). Let us further assume that the function of marginal utility of the commodity (*A*) is *F*( ) for the former possessor and *J*( ) for the latter, and that the corresponding functions of the commodity (*B*) are *f*( ) and *j*( ) respectively. Then the exchange is continued up to the point where

$$\frac{F(a-x)}{f(y)} = \frac{J(x)}{j(b-y)} \tag{3}$$

x and *y* denote here the number of the exchanged units of (*A*) and (*B*) respectively.

But we have here only a single equation between two

unknown quantities. The problem is consequently indeterminate; it has an infinite number of solutions. It could even appear as if, for each value of x, a y belonging to it could be found, and vice versa. This, however, is not so, because, as can easily be seen, the limiting condition must be added, that each of the exchanging persons ought to exchange with profit or at least without loss. The possible solutions consequently lie between two limits (margin pairs of x and y), in which cases the one or the other of the contracting parties has no profit at all (but also no loss). To determine these limits, when the functions of marginal utility are given on both sides, is a problem of the integral calculus. Let us think of the planned exchange as split up into an infinite number of partial exchanges, so that each time infinitesimal quantities, dx and dy, are exchanged against each other. If, then, the original possessor of commodity (A) gains nothing when he gives dx of (A) in exchange for dy of (B), the ratio $\dfrac{F(a - x)}{f(y)}$ of the marginal utilities to him of (A) and (B) must be the inverse of $\dfrac{dx}{dy}$. We therefore obtain each time

$$F(a - x) \cdot dx = f(y) \cdot dy$$

or, if we add up from zero to x and y on both sides,

$$\int_0^x F(a - x)dx = \int_0^y f(y)\, dy$$

in which case the upper limits must satisfy the integral of the equation (3).

Both these integrals, as can easily be seen, represent, for the possessor of (A), *the total utility* of the quantity of the commodity (A) given in exchange, and of the quantity of the commodity (B) taken in exchange, respectively. If, therefore, these functions of the total utility, now found by integration, are expressed by $\phi(\ )$ and $\psi(\ )$ respectively, we get

$$\phi(a) - \phi(a - x) = \psi(y)$$

By this equation, in combination with equation (3), the values in question of x and y can be determined.

In the same way, if the analogous functions in respect of the possessor of (B) are expressed by χ and ω, the other limit of the possible proportions of exchange is given by

$$\chi(x) = \omega(b) - \omega(b - y)$$

always in combination with (3). Between the limits thus determined, every proportion of exchange must be declared possible.

In order to make the foregoing a little clearer by an example,
we may be allowed to make the simplifying assumption that
for *both* the exchanging persons (which we will call A and B),
the functions of marginal utility of the same commodity are
identical, so that $J(\ )$ is identical with $F(\ )$ and $j(\ )$ with $f(\ )$,
and their values depend *only* on the possessed or exchanged
quantity of goods, not on the personal dispositions or other
circumstances of A and B. Moreover, let us suppose that both
functions of marginal utility can be replaced by approximating
formulae of the first degree, $\alpha - 2\beta x$ and $\alpha' - 2\beta'y$, *and this
over the whole sphere of the problem*, which, of course, as
already mentioned, can only be the case under special circumstances. The equation (3) then turns into

$$\frac{\alpha - 2\beta(a - x)}{\alpha' - 2\beta'y} = \frac{\alpha - 2\beta x}{\alpha' - 2\beta'(b - y)}$$

and if here numerator is added to numerator and denominator
to denominator, each of these fractions becomes

$$= \frac{\alpha - \beta a}{\alpha' - \beta'b} = \frac{F(a) + F(0)}{f(b) + f(0)}$$

The ratio of the marginal utilities of the two goods, when
equilibrium has been attained, is therefore, under the above
assumptions, constant, independently of the values of x and y
concerned, and equal to the proportion of the *average* marginal
utilities of the quantities possessed. In whatever proportion the
commodities here change hands by a repeated exchange, the
last exchange which leads to equilibrium will always take place
in the same proportion.[1]

Suppose that A has 10 oxen and B has 100 sheep, and that
the marginal utility of oxen is expressed by $200 - 10x$, and
the marginal utility of sheep by $10 - 0\cdot1y$. That is to say, in
B's estimation, if he does not yet possess on ox, one ox is
worth 200 (e.g. 200 *Marks*, if the value of 1 *Mark* is regarded
as constant); for every ox which he takes in exchange, the
value of an ox will seem to him 10 (10 *Marks*) less, etc. The
same is true for A, so that he, if he still possesses all the 10 oxen,

[1] This circumstance was put forward by Launhardt (p. 37) as a general rule,
but it is evidently only valid under the above simplifying assumptions, which
are, however, by no means general.

estimates the value of 1 ox as 100 *Marks* only, but for every ox which he gives in exchange he will increase that value by 10 *Marks*, etc. In an analogous way the same is true of the marginal utility function of the sheep.[1] Properly speaking, we are dealing here with oxen in the same way as with sheep, namely as optionally divisible continuous quantities; so that it would be more correct to say that B estimates the first fraction, for example the first hundredth of an ox, as worth 2 *Marks*, the second hundredth as worth 1 *Mark* 90 *Pfennig*, etc.

We therefore have here

$$\alpha = 200, \quad 2\beta = 10, \quad \alpha' = 10, \quad 2\beta' = 0 \cdot 1$$

When equilibrium has been attained, we necessarily get

$$\frac{200 - 10(10 - x)}{10 - 0 \cdot 1y} = \frac{200 - 10x}{10 - 0 \cdot 1(100 - y)}$$

or, written in a shorter way,

$$\frac{100 + 10x}{10 - 0 \cdot 1y} = \frac{200 - 10x}{0 \cdot 1y}, \text{ consequently, } = \frac{30}{1}$$

as follows by the addition of numerator to numerator and denominator to denominator. The last fraction expresses the constant and on both sides equal proportion of the marginal utilities in case of equilibrium, and consequently also the proportion in which both commodities are *at last* always exchanged.

The above equation finally reduces itself, as can easily be found, to

$$10x + 3y = 200$$

This equation must always be fulfilled after the exchange has taken place, but otherwise, within the above-mentioned limits, all possible proportions of exchange can occur. In order to determine these limits, we put, as we have already ascertained, supposing that A exchanges without any profit,

$$\int_0^x (100 + 10x)dx = \int_0^y (10 - 0 \cdot 1y)dy$$

[1] To the possessor of the sheep, a single sheep would at the beginning appear to have no value at all. One must therefore presume that the hundredth sheep can neither be fed nor consumed nor used by him in another way. The possibility of some other exchange we exclude on principle. For A, on the contrary, the value of one sheep is initially 10 *Marks*, etc.

or

$$100x + 5x^2 = 10y - \frac{y^2}{20}$$

But if B exchanges without profit,

$$\int_0^x (200 - 10x)dx = \int_0^y 0\cdot 1ydy$$

or

$$200x - 5x^2 = \frac{y^2}{20}$$

each time in conjunction with the equation

$$10x + 3y = 200$$

From these equations we obtain for the one limit

$$x = 6\sqrt{5} - 10; \quad y = 100 - 20\sqrt{5}$$
$$= 3\cdot42 \qquad\qquad = 55\cdot28$$

and for the other limit

$$x = 20 - 6\sqrt{10}; \quad y = 20\sqrt{10}$$
$$= 1\cdot03 \qquad\qquad = 63\cdot24$$

The possible proportion of exchange will consequently be able to fluctuate between about 1 ox against 61 sheep and $3\cdot4$ oxen against only 55 sheep (or on an average 1 ox against about 16 sheep). In the first case B, and in the second A, will have exchanged without any profit (but also without loss).

As the proportion of marginal utility amounts in the end always to '1 ox worth 30 sheep,' it could, for example, be supposed that both the contracting parties had from the beginning agreed to exchange in just this proportion. One would then have, beside the equation

$$10x + 3y = 200$$

which is always fulfilled, the equation

$$x = 30y$$

so that $x = 2$ and $y = 60$; that is to say, A gives 2 oxen to B and gets in return 60 sheep. It is easy to show that the gain of utility then becomes *the same* on both sides, namely 200 (*Marks*).[1]

But if, for instance, B knows how to direct the proportions of exchange to his advantage, 3 oxen against only 56⅔ sheep (on an average 1 ox against 19 sheep) might be given by A. But A might perhaps not be inclined to do this in a single exchange, for although at first he values 1 ox as equivalent to 10 sheep, this proportion of marginal utility would have risen to '1 ox worth 30 sheep' after the exchange, so that the transaction could appear to him as of doubtful use, though in reality it would bring him no loss according to our assumptions.

But supposing that he was first expected to exchange 1 ox for 13 sheep, then a second ox for 17⅔ sheep, then ½ ox for 11 sheep and finally another ½ ox for 15 sheep, then there would remain for him *after* each exchange respectively a proportion of exchange between sheep and oxen of more than 1 : 13, 1 : 17⅔, 1 : 22 and finally of just 1 : 30, so that each single exchange would have to seem to him undoubtedly profitable, although he has in fact finally exchanged just 3 oxen for not quite 57 sheep.

In the case of isolated exchange, too, of course, a kind of maximum problem is solved, for each of the exchanging persons strives after the greatest possible profit and is inclined to continue the exchange until he can derive no further profit from it. But since the whole problem is indeterminate, one can speak of a definite solution only when new conditions are added.

Such a condition would be, for instance, to determine the quantities of goods which are to be exchanged in such a way that the gain of utility attained *by both the contracting parties together*, in other words, approximately the 'economic' profit, becomes the greatest possible one. It is self-evident that, if this aim is attained by the exchange which has taken place, the

[1] For A's total utility increases by

$$10y - \frac{y^2}{20} - 100x - 5x^2 = 200$$

and B's by

$$200x - 5x^2 - \frac{y^2}{20} = 200.$$

This characteristic feature also was noticed by Launhardt. It is valid, however, only under the above-made assumptions, which, as he asserts, are by no means 'to be regarded as approximately right,' but at best permissible by way of example.

proportion of marginal utility of both commodities on each side must be the same and that consequently the equation (3) must be fulfilled, for otherwise the exchange could always, as we have seen, be continued with a gain of utility *on both sides*, so that the gain of utility already attained could not possibly be the greatest possible one. But this does not mean that the solution of this problem belongs to the *possible* solutions mentioned above.

The mathematical treatment of this problem is very simple; one has only to express that the sum of the gains of utility on both sides, or, which is the same, the sum of the total utility attained on both sides

$$\phi(a - x) + \psi(y) + \chi(x) + \omega(b - y)$$

is to be as great as possible. Since x and y are here independent of each other, one must consequently have at the same time

$$\frac{d}{dx}[\phi(a - x) + \chi(x)] = 0$$

or, differently expressed,

$$F(a - x) = J(x)$$

and

$$\frac{d}{dy}[\psi(y) + \omega(b - y)] = 0 \text{ or } f(y) = j(b - y)$$

By this the equation (3) is obviously exactly fulfilled; but whether the pair of values of x and y, so determined, really lies within the limits of the possible exchange, has still to be decided.

The matter becomes especially simple, if, as in our chosen example, the marginal utility functions are conceived as identical on both sides, $F(\ )$ with $J(\ )$ and $f(\ )$ with $j(\ )$. In this case the equations

$$F(a - x) = J(x) \text{ and } f(b - y) = j(y)$$

are obviously fulfilled by $x = \dfrac{a}{2}$ and $y = \dfrac{b}{2}$; and in consequence

of the general characteristics of the marginal utility functions, it is clear that they can have no other (real) solutions. In other words, the greatest possible total utility is attained under these assumptions if the existing supply is simply distributed in equal shares between both the exchanging persons. This, by the way, is evident.

In our example, therefore, A would give 5 oxen to B and would get 50 sheep for them. Thereby the conditioning equation

$$10x + 3y = 200$$

is indeed fulfilled and the proportion of marginal utility turns out to be such that 1 ox is estimated on both sides as equal to 30 sheep, as was required by the theory. But this exchange lies far beyond the possible limits. Indeed, it would bring to A a loss instead of a profit, and is consequently excluded, if each of the exchanging persons pursues his own profit. (Compare, moreover, section 5.)

In what has gone before we set out from the hypothesis that the commodities which are to be exchanged cannot *replace* each other in any way, so that the marginal utility only depends on the possession of the commodity in question, but not on the possession of the other. In reality, however, this is not always, and perhaps never wholly, the case. In our example, therefore, it cannot in fact be without significance for the valuation of an ox, whether the possessor in question has or has not, besides a certain number of oxen, also sheep. Therefore it would correspond more to reality if, as Edgeworth[1] has done, one conceived the total utility for A of oxen and sheep together as a general function U of x and y, whereby the partial derivatives of U in relation to x and y (taken positively) obviously express the marginal utility for A of the oxen and sheep respectively. If V is the corresponding function for B, one obtains as a conditioning equation of the exchange (called 'contract curve' by Professor Edgeworth) the very elegant expression

$$\frac{dU}{dx} : \frac{dU}{dy} = \frac{dV}{dx} : \frac{dV}{dy}$$

which turns into the above equation (3), as soon as one is allowed to suppose that

$$U = \phi(a - x) + \psi(y)$$

and

$$V = \chi(x) + \omega(b - y)$$

[1] Cf. Marshall, *Principles of Economics*, Appendix, note XII.

that is to say, when the utility (total utility as well as marginal utility) of each commodity only depends on the possessed quantity of *this* commodity.

5—Exchange in the open market

We have treated the individual exchange in such great detail merely in order to be able to demonstrate by means of a simple example the most important fundamental principles of the exact manner of treatment, not for the sake of its practical importance, for this is small. In modern economic life almost all proportions of exchange are determined by the open market or indirectly by its influence.

In the market, however, an element is added which causes the problem which we just now had to declare indeterminate, to appear relatively determinate. Jevons calls this the *law of indifference*, but it is in fact nothing other than *competition*, the mutual competition of buyers and sellers. Under the influence of competition, as we are accustomed to say, only one price can rule on the market and in its neighbourhood, so that all partial exchanges are carried out approximately in one and the same proportion of exchange.

It would, of course, be possible, and indeed it occurs quite often, that the one or the other party in the market attains in the first instance by an initial restraint a price higher than the one which later proves compatible with the general situation of the market; but then there is always the danger that some members of the party, cleverly using this good opportunity, might dispose of their whole stock at this artificially raised price, with the result that for the others the situation of the market would become so bad that in the end this procedure would bring them more loss than profit. It is just this latter circumstance that marks the principal difference between the market and the individual exchange. If one tries to avoid this danger by agreements in respect of the quantities of goods to be sold and bought, that is to say by cartels, etc., the conditions of the individual exchange are more or less repeated.

We simply suppose here as a fact that on the market one price or a proportion of exchange between every two commodities establishes itself within a short time for each commodity in which afterwards the bulk of the transactions are done. And supposing only two commodities are present on the market and are going to be exchanged against each other, let us set ourselves the task of finding out the proportion of exchange at which equilibrium is attained on the market. If this proportion is $1 : p$ so that p units of the commodity (B) are given against one unit of the commodity (A), *each* of the exchanging persons will exchange in just this proportion and he will, exactly as in the case of fixed prices treated above, exchange up to the point where *for him* the proportion of the marginal utility of the commodity (A) to that of the commodity (B) becomes $p : 1$. Let us suppose that there are m possessors of the commodity (A) and n possessors of the commodity (B), each of whom we suppose, for the sake of simplicity, to be originally provided with only one of the two commodities. If we then express the marginal utility function of the commodity (A) for the different possessors of this commodity and for those of the commodity (B) by $F_1(\ )$, $F_2(\ ) \ldots F_m(\ )$ and $J_1(\ )$, $J_2(\ ) \ldots J_n(\ )$ respectively, and the marginal utility function of the commodity (B) for those possessors by $f_1(\ )$, $f_2(\ ) \ldots f_m(\ )$ and $j_1(\ )$, $j_2(\ ) \ldots j_n(\ )$ respectively, we get the system of equations:

$$
\left.
\begin{aligned}
\frac{F_1(a_1 - x_1)}{f_1(y_1)} &= \frac{y_1}{x_1} = p & \qquad \frac{J_1(x_1')}{j_1(b_1 - y_1')} &= \frac{y_1'}{x_1'} = p \\[2mm]
\frac{F_2(a_2 - x_2)}{f_2(y_2)} &= \frac{y_2}{x_2} = p & \qquad \frac{J_2(x_2')}{j_2(b_2 - y_2')} &= \frac{y_2'}{x_2'} = p \\[1mm]
\cdots \quad & \cdots \quad \cdots \quad & \cdots \quad \cdots \quad & \cdots \\[1mm]
\frac{F_m(a_m - x_m)}{f_m(y_m)} &= \frac{y_m}{x_m} = p & \qquad \frac{J_n(x_n')}{j_n(b_n - y_n')} &= \frac{y_n'}{x_n'} = p
\end{aligned}
\right\} \quad (4)
$$

in which a_1, $a_2 \ldots$ express quantities initially owned by the various possessors of the commodity (A), x_1, y_1, x_2, y_2, $\ldots$ express the quantity of (A) and (B) which each of them has given and taken in exchange respectively, and b_1, $b_2 \ldots$; x_1', y_1', x_2', $y_2' \ldots$ have the same significance in relation to the original possessors of (B).[1]

[1] Since the x_1, $x_2, \ldots$; y_1, $y_2, \ldots$ generally become different from the x_1', $x_2', \ldots$; y_1', $y_2', \ldots$ one must, of course, suppose that every possessor generally does business with *several* possessors of the commodities desired by him.

We have here, therefore, $2m + 2n$ equations. To these, two other equations have to be added, which tell us that the sum of the quantity of goods given in exchange and the quantity of goods taken in exchange must be equal for each of the two commodities; consequently

$$x_1 + x_2 + \ldots + x_m = x_1' + x_2' + \ldots + x_n' \qquad (5)$$

and

$$y_1 + y_2 + \ldots + y_m = y_1' + y_2' + \ldots + y_n' \qquad (6)$$

Of the two latter equations, however, each can be derived from the other with the help of the equations (4).[1] We consequently obtain altogether $2(m + n) + 1$ equations, which are independent of each other, or just as many as the number of the unknown magnitudes: $x_1 \ldots x_m$, $y_1 \ldots y_m$, $x_1' \ldots x'$, $y_1' \ldots y_n$ and p. Our problem is consequently theoretically solved. We will undertake the discussion of these equations and their discontinuities later on, when we deal with supply and demand.

It would simplify matters somewhat if we were permitted to suppose that the marginal utility function of one or the other commodity depended *only* on the quantity possessed, but not on the personal disposition of the exchanging persons, so that the functions $F_1 \ldots F_m$, $J_1 \ldots J_n$ could approximately be replaced by one and the same function, perhaps $F(\ )$, just as the functions $f_1 \ldots f_m$, $j_1 \ldots j_n$ can all be replaced by the function $f(\ )$. If, further, we suppose what seems more doubtful still, however, and can indeed apply only to one special case, namely that $F(\ )$ and $f(\ )$ can both be expressed sufficiently exactly *for the whole field of this problem* by one approximating function of the first degree, $\alpha - \beta x$ and $\gamma - \delta y$ respectively, then we obtain by the addition of numerator to numerator and denominator to denominator in the equations (4) and with the help of (5) and (6)

$$p = \frac{(m+n)\alpha - \beta(a_1 + a_2 + \ldots + a_m)}{(m+n)\gamma - \delta(b_1 + b_2 + \ldots + b_n)} = \frac{\alpha - \beta \dfrac{A}{m+n}}{\gamma - \delta \dfrac{B}{m+n}}$$

[1] For one has, as can easily be seen,

$$\frac{y_1 + y_2 + \ldots + y_m}{x_1 + x_2 + \ldots + x_m} = p = \frac{y_1' + y_2' + \ldots + y_n'}{x_1' + x_2' + \ldots + x_n'}$$

provided that by A and B we express the size of the existing total supply of (A) and (B). The equilibrium price appears here, therefore, as about the proportion of the *average* marginal utilities of the commodities (A) and (B), or of those marginal utilities which would result if the existing supply were distributed equally amongst all exchanging persons. The equilibrium price depends only on the number of barterers and on the size of the total stock, but not on its original distribution. When p is already determined in this way, one obtains the other unknown magnitudes of the problem, x_1, x_2, etc., very simply by an equation of the first degree in each case.

This observation, which is at any rate interesting, was made by Launhardt. It is open to doubt whether any practical importance can be attached to it. As we have already several times remarked, this rule can only be generally valid, i.e. valid for all forms of functions, if it is a question of very small deviations, that is to say, if *all* exchanging persons are from the outset or by previous exchange in possession of approximately *equal* quantities of the same commodity, so that the marginal utility of the commodity (A) as well as that of the commodity (B) is already *nearly equal* for all of them. This, however, will not often come about in reality; for even if the marginal utility *function* were identical throughout, the amounts of property would nevertheless be different. From this it follows that this function can indeed be replaced by a series of different approximating functions, but not by one and the same formula,[1] as the validity of the rule requires.

The treatment of the problem of exchange given above derives from Walras. Jevons, who has also availed himself of the mathematical method, but in a less correct way, believed that he could summarize the solution in *two* equations by regarding all possessors of the one as well as of the other commodity as a *trading body*. According to Jevons, for each of these trading bodies, in respect of each of the commodities, a kind of collective marginal utility holds good, which can be regarded as a function of the possessed or acquired *total* supply. If A and B are the total supplies of the commodities (A) and (B), and X and Y the exchanged total quantities of these, and if the mentioned collective marginal utility is

[1] Considered geometrically, it is represented by a curve which can nearly always be replaced by a *broken* line, but not by one and the same *straight* line.

expressed by $F(\ )$, $J(\ )$, $f(\ )$ and $j(\ )$ respectively,[1] we obtain

$$\frac{F(A - X)}{f(Y)} = \frac{Y}{X} = \frac{J(X)}{j(B - Y)}.$$

In this case the proportion of exchange to be determined is of course given by $\dfrac{Y}{X}$.

But Jevons never says clearly what is really meant by this collective marginal utility of a *trading body*, and it seems as if he himself had not formed a sufficiently clear idea of it. The marginal utility of a commodity for a trading body can scarcely be anything else but the average marginal utility, the arithmetical mean, or else any mean of the individual marginal utilities of its members. But neither is it clear how the proportion of exchange can depend on this average marginal utility in the way Jevons demands, nor can one understand how it could be conceived as a function of the size of the possessed total supply, since the average marginal utility in fact also depends on the distribution of this supply and, what is more, on the distribution *after* the exchange, which is still unknown.[2]

If the members of the party, instead of operating each for himself on the market, were to buy and sell on joint account, in other words, if they formed a real trading body instead of a trading body which was only feigned, then we could indeed speak of their collective marginal utility; but then the reciprocal competition would be excluded. We should still be in the sphere of isolated exchange and there would be no fixed equilibrium price.

Jevons's solution is therefore insufficient, although he has correctly grasped the fundamental idea of the theory.

[1] In Jevons's book these signs are represented by $\phi_1(\ )$, $\phi_2(\ )$, $\psi_1(\ )$ and $\psi_2(\ )$.

[2] Jevons's formula could be applied in one case only, namely when the marginal utility function concerned may be replaced by an approximating function of the first degree which is identical for all members of the market party in question. (It is a somewhat less special case than the one mentioned above, where this function must be identical for the members of *both* parties.) Then, as can easily be seen, the arithmetical mean of all the marginal utility values would only be dependent on the acquired or remaining total supply of the community concerned and on the number of the possessors in question. Jevons's formula, which in that case would probably assume the form

$$\frac{m\alpha - \beta(A - X)}{m\gamma - \delta Y} = \frac{Y}{X} = \frac{n\alpha' - \beta'X}{n\gamma' - \delta'(B - Y)}$$

would then indeed be sufficient to determine the proportion of exchange at which equilibrium rules on the market.

But if with Walras one takes, instead of the exchanged total quantities themselves, their *proportion*, namely the average proportion of exchange, as the independent variable, it is indeed possible, as we shall soon see, to unite the equations of the exchange in one single formula, which is then nothing other than the mathematical expression for the equality of supply and demand.

In the case of exchange in the open market also, as well as in the cases treated previously, a maximum problem is solved; but only in the sense that each of the exchanging persons (and consequently all of them together) obtains the greatest possible gain of utility which can be attained by him (or them) *at the price fixed on the market*. On the other hand, this would obviously not be the case if a uniform price were fixed in advance in some other way, e.g. by governmental order. That being so, only one market party, the one not favoured, could exchange until saturation was reached; but at no time could all the members of the other party, or perhaps even a single member, sell such a great amount of their goods as would be profitable for them at this price. Equilibrium on the market would then be impossible, since the supply of the favoured commodity would always exceed the demand.[1]

It can, however, *not* be asserted that the gain of utility attained by all the exchanging persons together is necessarily *smaller* in the latter case than in the case of entirely free competition.

Generally speaking, of course, this will prove true; for if the fixed price deviates very much from the equilibrium price, the exchanged quantities of goods become in the end so small that the gain of utility on both sides, too, lags behind the gain of utility attainable in the case of free competition. Up to a certain limit, however, the profit of the favoured party is increased with each such shifting of the price; and it cannot generally be proved that the profit of the other party decreases thereby in a corresponding degree.

Still less can it be asserted that the distribution of the commodities which is most favourable economically, that is to say, the greatest possible general satisfaction, arises from free competition. If this problem is conceived in the absolute sense,

[1] Of other selling possibilities and of the production of the goods concerned, no account is taken here.

its solution, as can easily be seen, requires that the marginal utility of all exchanging persons should become the same *in relation to each separate commodity*.[1] But this situation will quite often lie beyond the limits of the possible exchange, as it would bring to some of the exchanging persons loss instead of profit. This, however, does not prevent the problem from being solved in the relative sense, that is to say, in so far as it is compatible with the fundamental condition of exchange. But this could obviously only happen if the individual transactions were carried out at different prices, instead of at the single joint price required by free competition.[2]

But after all, the question of the most suitable distribution of goods forms a problem which is entirely different from that of the theory of exchange. For it supposes that utility or satisfaction can also be compared for *different persons*, whilst the theory of exchange only proceeds from the possibility of comparing the utilities of different commodities *for one and the same person*; which is quite a different matter.

6—Exchange of several goods. Indirect exchange

If three or more commodities come to be exchanged on the market, not only do our formulae become, in a corresponding degree, more complex, but quite a new phenomenon appears, which is of the greatest importance from the economic point of

---

[1] Cf. the above treatment of this problem in respect of two exchanging persons.

[2] Launhardt reproached Walras with 'great error' in supposing that 'what is generally best would most certainly be reached by the natural effect of the rule of free competition.' As far as I know, however, Walras has never asserted this, although he expresses himself a little incautiously upon this subject.

However, it is precisely at this point that Launhardt himself goes seriously astray; for he believes that he has proved that 'in the case of an exchange at equilibrium prices the greatest profit, economically speaking, is reached, if we assume that the exchange takes place in one single transaction' (loc. cit., p. 38). This is completely wrong. What Launhardt has proved in the passage in question (p. 28) is something quite different: that for each of the exchanging persons, and consequently for all of them together, as was shown above, the highest satisfaction attainable *at this price* arises from exchange at equilibrium price. But he has not shown, and it is not generally true, that this total satisfaction would be greater than that which could arise from any other price. This is quite obvious if we suppose, for example, that the marginal utility in respect of *both* commodities for one of the exchanging persons (or parties) is so small that the gain of utility to this person (or party) cannot be taken into consideration at all. Then it is clear that the total gain also becomes greater in proportion as the other party is able to direct the price to its advantage.

view, namely the *indirect exchange*, which consists in the fact that a commodity is taken in exchange, not in order to be kept and consumed, but in order to be again given in exchange.

Suppose, for example, that three commodities (A), (B) and (C) are present on the market, which are to be simultaneously exchanged for one another. It could now seem as if each possessor of the commodity (A) would simply relinquish part of his possession of (A) against a certain quantity of (B) and another part of (A) against a certain quantity of (C), according to the law of the proportionality of the corresponding marginal utilities—and similarly with the possessors of (B) and (C)—so that the quantity of (A) given by the possessors of (A) to the possessors of (B) would constitute the *remuneration* for the quantity of (B) obtained, etc. This, however, will generally *not* be the case, for a general equilibrium on the market would thereby not yet be attained. Rather, the direct exchange is almost always followed by an indirect one, since at least some of the possessors of (A) derive their advantage by exchanging against each other certain quantities of (B), in order to exchange them afterwards for corresponding quantities of (C), or vice versa. An analogous operation can, of course, also be undertaken by the possessors of (B) or of (C), or simultaneously by the members of the different parties.

The same result can also be attained with the help of *credit or money*. The possessors of (A) then surrender certain quantities of (A) to the possessors of (B) without direct remuneration, or for money. On the other hand, they obtain from the possessors of (C) a corresponding quantity of (C) without direct remuneration, or for the money which they have just received from the possessors of (B). Finally, the possessors of (B) surrender a corresponding quantity of (B) to the possessors of (C) for just this sum of money, or against the claim which the possessors of (A) have on the possessors of (B) and which they have transferred to the possessors of (C); so that either the money finally returns to the starting-point or the claims are discharged. The result will be the same as in the case originally supposed, save that the quantities of (B), which previously went through the hands of the possessors of (A) as middlemen, are now transferred directly to the possessors of (C).

If credit and money transactions as well as wholesale trade are excluded for any reason, then the quantities of goods which are surrendered on both sides—one of one sort for one of another—must certainly be exchanged directly. But then the three proportions of exchange between (A) and (B), between (B) and (C) and between (C) and (A) will stand in no relation whatsoever; so that if, for instance, in the trade between the possessors of (A) and (B), two units of (A) are given for every unit of (B), and in the exchange between (B) and (C), three units of (B) are given for every unit of (C), then, in the exchange between (C) and (A), perhaps five, seven, or any number of units of (A) whatsoever, can be exchanged for each unit of (C), whilst in the case of free exchange, exactly six units of (A) would have to be given for every unit of (C).

Or vice versa. If we suppose that the proportions of exchange of the three commodities are dependent on each other, so that one of them is always determined, in the simple way indicated above, by the other two, then we cannot make the further stipulation that the quantities of goods finally sold should *pay* for each other, or should be directly exchanged against each other. The problem would then be *over*determinate.

We are here obviously confronted with one of the most important questions of the theory of exchange. The 'exchange between three' forms, so to speak, a connecting link, which leads from the state of primitive exchange to that of developed economy, where two producers or other possessors of commodities, as we know from experience, almost never exchange their goods directly. A will give his commodity to B, B will give the one he possesses to C, C his to D, etc., until the chain is completed, usually by way of various ramifications.

In order to simplify the mathematical treatment of this problem as far as possible, it is perhaps best to unite the different possessors of commodities not in several, but *in one single group*, each of whose members is already from the outset conceived as possessor of certain quantities of all these goods, and therefore, on the assumption of only three commodities, as the possessor of all three. Initially, one or two of these quantities can, of course, be zero.[1]

Suppose the number of all the exchanging persons is n.

[1] The problem of exchange of *two* commodities also could, of course, have been treated in this way. This would express the more general case, where each of the exchanging persons at first possess *both* commodities, and according to the level of prices acts as buyer of the one commodity and seller of the other, *or vice versa*.

One of them has at the outset the quantities a_r, b_r and c_r of the commodities (A), (B) and (C) respectively, where r is an optional index number. After the completed exchange, he will possess the quantities $a_r + x_r$, $b_r + y_r$ and $c_r + z_r$ in which at least one of the magnitudes x_r, y_r, z_r must be *negative* and therefore expresses a quantity of goods *given in exchange* instead of a quantity of goods taken in exchange. But also *two* of these magnitudes could be negative, if the person concerned had originally possessed (at least) two of the three commodities, and had given away certain quantities of both for each quantity of the third commodity.

If we further suppose that the equilibrium prices of the three commodities, measured according to an optional standard, are p_a, p_b and p_c,[1] the principle of thrift (the principle of the greatest possible profit for everyone) demands that the possessor in question exchange up to the point at which, for him, the marginal utilities of the three commodities stand in the same proportion as their prices. We consequently have, if the marginal utilities of the three commodities for him are expressed by $F_r(\ )$, $G_r(\ )$ and $H_r(\ )$

$$F_r(a_r + x_r): G_r(b_r + y_r): H_r(c_r + z_r) = p_a: p_b: p_c \qquad (7)$$

This amounts to two independent equations.

For each of the exchanging persons there exist two similar equations or, altogether, $2n$ equations.

We have now in addition to express the fact that for each possessor the amount realized by the goods taken in exchange is equal to the amount realized by the quantity of goods which he gave for them from his original stock of goods. We thus obtain, as can easily be seen, n equations of the type

$$x_r p_a + y_r p_b + z_r p_c = 0 \qquad (8)$$

But finally, three other equations must be considered here—to the effect that the algebraic sum of the (positive) quantities of *each* of the three commodities taken in exchange and the

[1] Obviously, any one of the commodities could itself be conceived as the standard of value, in which case the price of this commodity would $= 1$. For the sake of symmetry, however, we have adopted a different standard of value, as in fact, in most cases, agrees best with reality; for even if two commodities are exchanged for each other in a simple way by reciprocal credit between two business-men, their value is initially almost always reckoned in money.

(negative) quantities given in exchange must be *zero*. We have therefore in addition

$$
\left.\begin{aligned}
x_1 + \ldots + x_r + \ldots + x_n &= 0 \\
y_1 + \ldots + y_r + \ldots + y_n &= 0 \\
z_1 + \ldots + z_r + \ldots + z_n &= 0
\end{aligned}\right\} \tag{9}
$$

Of these equations, however, only two are independent, since the third can always be obtained from the others with the help of the n equations (8) (by their addition), as can easily be seen.

For the same number of unknowns, namely the $3n$ quantities $x_1 \ldots x_n,\ y_1 \ldots y_n,\ z_1 \ldots z_n$ and the two proportions of the three prices, we obtain therefore altogether $3n + 2$ equations; for instance

$$
\frac{p_b}{p_a} \text{ and } \frac{p_c}{p_a}, \text{ by which also } \frac{p_c}{p_b} = \frac{p_c}{p_a} \Big/ \frac{p_b}{p_a}
$$

is then determined.

The absolute level of these prices themselves cannot, of course, be ascertained here, since they were reckoned according to an optional measure which cannot be exactly determined.

If, on the contrary, we had chosen one of the commodities, e.g. (A), as the standard of value, so that we had $p_a = 1$, p_b and p_c could, of course, be determined. They would then represent the price of (B) and of (C) respectively, expressed in terms of (A).

As we see, no difference is made here between the possessors of different commodities. It would be quite easy, however, to do this. We should then—assuming that, for instance, each person possesses at first only *one* commodity—have to divide the exchanging persons into three groups, in which case, according to our notation, all initial quantities b and c in the first group, the quantities c and a in the second group, and a and b in the third group would be *zero*. The other way of dealing with this problem would be exactly the same as above. But if one wanted to introduce here at the same time the condition that the sum of the y's in the first group and the sum of the x's in the second group, multiplied by p_b and p_a respectively, should be *equal to one another* (from which it follows directly that the sum of the z's in the first group, multiplied by p_c, and the sum of the x's in the third group, multiplied by

p_a, must also be equal to one another as well as to the sum of the z's in the second group and the sum of the y's in the third group, multiplied by p_c and p_b respectively)—in other words, supposing that the transacting persons only obtain possession of the commodities by direct exchange—then the problem is *overdeterminate* and cannot be solved. We should then have not merely $3n + 2$, but $3n + 3$ equations, which would be independent of each other, whilst there are only $3n + 2$ unknown magnitudes to be determined.

On the other hand one could easily introduce the condition of direct exchange, if one conceived the three proportions of exchange between (A) and (B), between (A) and (C) and finally between (B) and (C) as *three magnitudes which are independent of each other*.[1] The unknowns of the problem would then be increased by one, and would then amount to $3n + 3$.

This is how Jevons treats the problem,[2] except that, as in the case of exchange between two commodities, he introduces the vague concept of the marginal utility of a 'trading body,' by which means he believes that he is able to reduce the number of equations to only $2 \times 3 = 6$.

But Jevons does not seem to have noticed that the state of equilibrium expressed by his equations excludes, in principle, the possibility of the wholesale trade as well as money and credit transactions, and that, if these are admitted, the equilibrium would immediately be disturbed afresh. He reminds us that the same pair of goods can only have one proportion of exchange in the same market, but he never mentions that in the case of a completely free exchange of three commodities there can only be two independent proportions of exchange (and generally in the case of n commodities only $n - 1$); indeed he treats these proportions of exchange as if all three would be independent.

Finally, so far as the question of the greatest possible profit is concerned, much the same applies here as in the case of exchange between two commodities only. Each party to the exchange attains, at the equilibrium prices fixed by free competition, the greatest possible profit attainable by him *at just these prices*. It is here specially to be remarked that, if initially only direct exchange is permitted, but subsequently the market

---

[1] In this case, the notation used above will have to be altered correspondingly.
[2] *Theory of Political Economy*, 2nd edition, p. 124 ff.

is entirely freed, each of the exchanging persons will acquire a greater profit by the wholesale trade or stock-exchange operations which then take place, and in this way the total profit also can become greater. But the state of equilibrium thus attained will generally be different from that which would occur if trade were entirely free *from the very beginning*. For this reason it cannot be asserted that in the case of entirely free trade a greater total profit can invariably be obtained than if, for instance, only direct exchange were allowed. It can, however, easily be seen that this must on the whole be the case, and the more so, the more the division of labour is already carried through—which means that fewer direct exchange transactions can occur at all.

7—Supply and demand

We are, of course, still very far from being able to give our equations hitherto formulated a practical application, or from being able to test them in this way. The bare *number* of equations required makes this impossible. To be able actually to formulate these equations, it would be necessary to know exactly the plans of every single consumer in regard to each of the different commodities and the size of the existing individual supplies, which is, of course, impossible.

Secondly, it was assumed in the foregoing that all the commodities to be exchanged are optionally divisible and that their consumption, in relation to a certain period of consumption, represents, even within the individual economy, a continuously variable magnitude.

Neither the one nor the other holds good in reality without qualification. In the case of several commodities, only a limited number of separate specimens can be used at a time in individual consumption. But even if the commodities are themselves optionally divisible, the consumption will in most cases only be able to vary by discontinuous steps; which renders a mathematical treatment of the above kind more difficult still, or makes it impossible.

But the case is different if we speak of the total sum of commodities which are exchanged on the market or consumed within the economic territory concerned. Firstly, the quantities of goods in question could then, as a rule, be much better determined statistically. Secondly—and this is nearly as important for an exact treatment—their total consumption, by virtue of the *law of great numbers*, will almost always be able to be regarded as a magnitude continuously varying, even if the individual consumption only changes by discontinuous steps. Jevons was therefore perfectly right in trying to unite the exchanging persons into groups or 'trading bodies'; only, as we have seen, not much can be done with the concept of *marginal utility* of such a group. But we attain our end if, as Walras did, we conceive the prices or proportions of exchange of the commodities as *variable* and, what is more, as the only independent variables of the problem, or—which comes to the same thing—if we consider the exchange procedure from the point of view of supply and demand.

Let us first of all return to the exchange of *two* commodities.

If we solve all equations (4) in relation to $x_1, y_1, x_2, y_2, \ldots$ x_1', y_1', etc., every x and y and every x' and y' can be regarded as functions of p, where p is conceived as *variable*, if we leave out of account for the time being the equations (5) and (6). In other words, whenever both commodities are exchanged in the proportion of $1 : p$, which in one way or another has been fixed in advance, then from every single possessor A_r of the commodity (A) comes a certain *supply* x_r of this commodity and with it also a certain *demand* y_r for the commodity (B), where x_r and y_r, each by itself, are functions of p, which must always stand to each other in the simple relation

$$\frac{y_r}{x_r} = p \text{ or } y_r = px_r$$

In the same way, from every possessor B_q of the commodity (B) comes a certain *supply* y_q' of the commodity (B) and a certain *demand* x_q' for the commodity (A). y_q' and x_q', too, are functions of p, and stand in the same relation to each other as above. This we express better by

$$\frac{x_q'}{y'} = \frac{1}{p} \text{ or } x_q' = \frac{1}{p} \cdot y_q' = \pi y_q', \quad \text{where } \pi = \frac{1}{p};$$

since all the x' express here supply and all the y' demand. p therefore denotes the price of the commodity (A) expressed in terms of (B); consequently $\dfrac{1}{p}$ or π denotes the price of the commodity (B) expressed in terms of (A).[1]

If now we add together all the x's and call the resulting sum X, then this sum expresses the total supply of the commodity (A). In the same way we obtain by addition of all the y's the total demand Y for the commodity (B).

In the same way Y', the sum of all the y', expresses the total supply of (B), and X', the sum of all the x', the total demand for (A).

All these magnitudes become, therefore, functions of p or of π, the prices of the commodities reciprocal to each other, and, what is more, generally constant functions, even if the individual supplies and demands only vary by steps. If p rises a little and π consequently falls, the magnitudes X, Y, X' and Y' will, as we know from experience, rise by a very small amount, and fall respectively; and vice versa, if p falls and π rises. X, therefore, is transformed into $X + dX$ (where dp and dX can also be negative) or into $X + \dfrac{d}{dp}X \cdot dp$, etc., if p changes into $p + dp$.

But this generally does not happen in such a way that with every shift of prices the possessors of (A) now increase or decrease their consumption of (B) by, perhaps, one hundredth each—which might not even be possible, according to the nature of the commodity (B). Most of them are probably not in the least disposed to increase or restrict their consumption of the goods concerned by the change in prices which has taken place.

---

1 We must here draw attention to some discontinuities of our functions previously laid down, which we have not discussed so far. Our equations of value

$$\frac{F(a - x)}{f(y)} = \frac{y}{x} = p$$

no longer have any significance if they cannot be satisfied by a positive y and by an x which is at the same time positive and smaller than a. If p has already become so small that x, and consequently y also, are zero, the above equations must, if p continues to decrease, be replaced by $x = 0$, $y = 0$; that is to say, the possessor in question no longer exchanges at all.

If, on the contrary, x becomes equal to a, p increasing, then the possessor will sell at this price his whole supply of (A). If the price is a little higher still, he will generally, even at this price, exchange his whole supply, but not more, since he does not possess any more of (A). Our equations must then in the first instance give way to the more simple relationships $x = a$, $y = pa$.

If, moreover, we consider the discontinuities of the individual consumption and demand, x and y can by no means be regarded as continuous functions of p.

But *some* of them, while the price was still p, were presumably just about to consume the commodity (B) not yet used, or, on the contrary, to give up partly or completely their consumption of (B). For these, the rise or reduction in price dp is, as it were, the drop which causes the vessel to overflow. These alter their consumption and, what is more, not by an infinitely small, but by a relatively considerable amount, which, however, will be very small in comparison with the consumption of the majority of the consumers. This on the whole will be unchanged.

Let us now consider the equations (5) and (6). The former reduces itself to

$$X = X' \tag{10}$$

and simply expresses the fact that supply and demand of the commodity (A) must be equal in the case of equilibrium of the prices. By this the equation (6), or

$$Y = Y' \tag{11}$$

is also fulfilled, since Y is obviously $= pX$ and $Y' = pX'$. Equality of supply and demand of the one commodity causes the same relation in respect of the other commodity. Using either of these equations, p can now be determined, if we have found out the forms of the functions X and X' or Y and Y'.

However, a more detailed examination shows that equality of supply and demand is indeed a *necessary*, but, at least from the theoretical point of view, not a *sufficient* condition for the equilibrium of the market, supposing the latter to be *stable*— if, that is to say, the proportion of exchange would automatically return to (approximately) the same position after an accidental shifting.

If, for instance, it is a matter of demand and supply of the commodity (A), it can generally be asserted that, if p [the price of (A) expressed in terms of (B)] increases, the demand for (A) always falls; if, on the contrary, p decreases, the demand for (A) will always increase.[1] If we could now be certain that, on

---

[1] Strictly speaking, however, this is generally only the case when the commodities (A) and (B) cannot replace each other, so that, as we have assumed above, the marginal utility of one of them depends simply on the quantity owned of this commodity or on the quantity acquired, and not at the same time on the quantity acquired or the quantity owned of the other commodity. But if both commodities can replace each other completely or partly, it is a different matter. Suppose, for instance, that (B) is wheat and (A) potatoes. If a possessor of wheat can cover with it the whole of his annual food requirements, but

the contrary, the supply of (A), at least near the equilibrium price found [i.e. the value of p, ascertained from (10) or (11)] would increase when the price rose, and would decrease when the price fell, then the stability of the equilibrium would obviously be secured; for in the case of an accidental deviation of the price upwards the supply would be greater than the demand; in the case of a deviation downwards, the demand would, on the contrary, exceed the supply; in both cases the inequality of supply and demand would necessarily drive back the price to approximately the earlier position.

But we know in regard to the supply of (A) that this magnitude, multiplied by the price of (A), represents the demand for (B) $(Y = pX)$.

If now the demand for (A) decreases when the price of (A), expressed in terms of (B), rises, then the demand for (B) must for the same reason diminish when the price of (B), expressed in terms of (A), rises, and consequently *increase* if the price of (A), expressed in terms of (B), rises. If therefore we put the demand for (A) or $X' = \phi(p)$ and the demand for (B) or $Y = \psi(p)$, then $\phi(p)$ is consequently a decreasing function (when p increases); $\psi(p)$, on the other hand, is an increasing function of p. We therefore obtain for the supply of (A) or X the expression

$$X = \frac{1}{p} \cdot \psi(p)$$

which product, for different values of p, can under certain circumstances increase with increasing p, but also decrease. If $\psi(p)$ increases more rapidly than p, this product increases; if $\psi(p)$, on the other hand, increases less rapidly than p, it decreases.

When the price rises, therefore, not only the demand but also the supply of the commodity in question can decrease. If, now,

potatoes are cheaper in proportion to their nutritive value, then he will probably exchange every year a certain quantity of wheat for the cheaper potatoes. But if now the price of potatoes (expressed in terms of wheat) were to fall still lower, he could first of all procure for himself the same quantity of potatoes in exchange for a *smaller* outlay of wheat. But since he thus keeps more wheat, his annual requirements in the matter of food could be even *more* than covered in this way. Therefore, if it is for him only a question of satisfying these requirements, he will be able to keep without loss a still greater quantity of wheat and content himself with a *smaller* quantity of potatoes, so that *his demand* for potatoes would finally *decrease with the falling price* instead of increasing.

the demand decreases more *rapidly* than the supply (and therefore, on the contrary, increases more rapidly when the price falls), the stability of the equilibrium is, as can easily be seen, even in these circumstances still secured. But there is nothing to prevent $\dfrac{\psi(p)}{p}$ from decreasing or increasing even more rapidly than $\phi(p)$, near the value of p in question, since supply and demand of the same commodity proceed from different persons and are consequently totally independent of each other.[1]

If this is the case, no real equilibrium of the price exists, but only a temporary equality of supply and demand; for as soon as the price moves even in the least degree upwards the demand will be greater than the supply and the price must consequently rise higher and higher, until the demand, decreasing, finally catches up with the decreasing supply once more. In the same way a small shift of the price downwards will cause the supply to exceed the demand, and leads therefore to lower and lower prices, until the demand, increasing, again catches up with the increasing supply.

In both cases equilibrium is finally reached, but the equilibrium price will in each case be a different one. Thus the further peculiarity arises, that not only one, but *two different* (stable) *states of equilibrium* of the market would theoretically be possible.

Walras, and Launhardt after him, have drawn supply and demand curves in hypothetical form. By this means the price is represented as abscissa of a right-angled system of coordinates, and the quantities of goods demanded or supplied as ordinates of the different curves. Mangoldt, by the way, in his *Grundriss der Volkswirtschaftslehre*, which was published in 1863, had already drawn similar curves, which, however, were eliminated by the editor of the later edition of his work.

I reproduce on the next page Launhardt's diagram, in which, certainly, the peculiarity mentioned above does not appear.[2] Here, for the sake of greater clarity, two of these curves are drawn *beneath* the axis of the abscissae. If p is zero, i.e. if the

---

[1] Of the production of goods no account is taken here, of course.

[2] For, in accordance with his assumptions repeatedly mentioned, a simple marginal utility function (in respect of each of the commodities) was drawn, identical for both parties. Here, of course, the curves can only have one single (real) point of intersection in common.

commodity (*A*) is to be had for nothing, everybody, and consequently the possessors of (*B*) also, will provide themselves with it until saturation is reached, but they will not desire an infinite quantity of it. The demand curve therefore cuts the axis of ordinates at a certain distance from zero. If *p* increases, the demand for (*A*) on the part of the possessors of (*B*) decreases, and at a certain price this demand becomes zero.

The demand curve for (*B*) would now follow a similar course if the abscissae represented, instead of the price of (*A*) expressed in terms of (*B*), the price of (*B*) expressed in terms of (*A*)—that is to say, if *π* were chosen as abscissa. But in that case the demand for the commodity (*B*) will only begin at a value of *p*

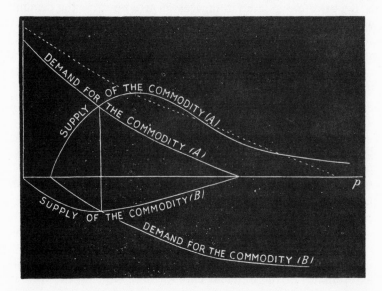

different from zero. From then on the demand for (*B*) increases as *p* increases, but will never be able to exceed a certain magnitude, namely the quantity of (*B*) which would be desired if *p* were infinite and consequently $\frac{1}{p}$ were $= 0$, that is to say, if the commodity (*B*) could be had for nothing. The demand curve for (*B*) therefore approaches asymptotically a straight line which is drawn at this distance parallel to the axis of the abscissae. The two curves mentioned so far, by the way, are absolutely independent according to our assumptions.

Each of the other two curves, on the contrary, is totally determined by the form of each of the previous curves. If the demand for (A) is given by the function $\phi(p)$, the supply of (B), as we have seen, is necessarily represented by $p \cdot \phi(p)$; in the same way $\frac{1}{p}\psi(p)$ expresses the supply of (A), if $\psi(p)$ expresses the demand for (B).

A direct consequence of this is, that the point of intersection of the supply and demand curves of (A) must lie vertically above the point of intersection of the supply and demand curves of (B). Both points of intersection determine one and the same value of p, namely the equilibrium price.

As regards the supply curve of the commodity (A) in particular, this has, as can be seen, a highest point and approaches afterwards the axis of the abscissae asymptotically. But although it is quite independent of the form of the demand curve of *the same* commodity, its intersection point with the latter can lie just as well on the right side of the highest point as on its left side (as in the figure). These two positions of the intersection point correspond to our two above-mentioned cases of stable equilibrium of the price. But this does not prevent these two curves from being able to have *more* than one point, and if so at least three points of intersection in common, as, for example, is shown by the dotted line [representing the demand for (A)] drawn in our figure.[1] If this is the case, the two extreme intersection points, as we can easily convince ourselves, determine prices of stable equilibrium. The middle intersection point, on the contrary, shows no real equilibrium of prices, as was mentioned above, but only a temporary equality of supply and demand.

This interesting result of the theory, which was first noticed by Walras, is impugned in the well-known work by Auspitz and Lieben,[2] who assert that 'the simultaneous validity of both demand curves [of the commodities (A) and (B)] is founded on assumptions which contradict each other.' In this case, the authors go on to argue, one would have to assume firstly that 'the prices or proportions of exchange of all other articles'

---

[1] In this case, the curves of the commodity (B) also would, of course, intersect at three points, lying vertically under the points of intersection of the curves of commodity (A).

[2] *Untersuchungen über die Theorie des Preises*, Preface, p. XXIII.

excluding the commodity (*B*) are constant against one another; and consequently, that the prices, on both sides, of all articles excluding the commodity (*A*), *but including the commodity* (*B*), are constant.

This objection seems to me to be unfounded. In Walras's presentation as well as in our examination up to now, no account is taken in principle of the presence of other articles on the market; it is assumed that the demand for (*A*) comes exclusively from the possessors of the commodity (*B*) and that the demand for (*B*) comes exclusively from the possessors of the commodity (*A*). But we do not at all need to confine ourselves to this purely abstract assumption. If we put instead of the commodity (*B*) the sum total of all commodities on the market excluding the commodity (*A*), or what comes to about the same, if by one of the two commodities we understand *money*, then, at variable money prices of the commodity (*A*), the demand for (*A*) (which now comes from all other possessors of goods or consumers) as well as the supply of (*A*) [which is now determined by the demand on the part of the possessors of (*A*) for all other commodities] will on the whole have to follow the same course as in the case of only two commodities which we have considered.

The reciprocal proportions of exchange or the money prices of the other commodities exercise their influence, of course; but all these prices can be regarded, *in otherwise unchanging circumstances*, as dependent on the money price of the commodity (*A*). A demand and a supply curve of (*A*), as well as supply and demand curves of *money* dependent on them [those of the possessors of (*A*)], will consequently really exist; the supply curve of (*A*) will, if one draws the variable money price of (*A*) as abscissa, have a highest point, and from there it will approach the axis of the abscissae asymptotically, etc. The existence of differently characterized intersection points between these curves, as well as the possibility of several intersection points simultaneously, cannot therefore, at least *a priori*, be denied. The former result can even be regarded as a well-attested fact.

If, to be sure, one assumes, as Auspitz and Lieben do, that the valuation of money on the part of all exchanging persons is constant, then the supply curve of every single commodity must indeed always take a rising course, and we cannot then speak of several intersection points of the curves. This assumption can indeed be made in some cases, but by no means in all.

Let us take a few concrete examples. If, while the yield of the harvest and the size of supplies remain constant, the prices of corn for the year are for any reason higher than usual, and if importation of corn is excluded, one can by no means declare *a priori* that the supply of this commodity must now grow. It may be that the farmers—hitherto perhaps obliged to deny themselves much—desire to be better fed, now that their income has risen, or else to increase their own consumption of corn. The supply of corn will then, on the contrary, *decrease*. This, of course, supposes that the valuation of money on the part of the farmers has now decreased considerably; otherwise the raised price would induce them to increase their supplies and consequently to restrict their own consumption.

Or let us take as the commodity to be considered, the so-called 'commodity labour.' It is quite a common complaint amongst well-to-do people, that in times of relatively high wages people 'do not want to work'; and this complaint is probably founded on fact. The worker allows himself more leisure than before if he is better paid, and the supply of labour decreases instead of increasing. At least, this is a *possible* consequence. But let it be repeated, this can happen only if we assume that the valuation of money on the part of the workers has decreased just because of their increased wages.

The *descending* part of the supply curve is consequently in both these cases cut by the demand curve (which always follows a descending course). If in these circumstances the two curves chance to run close together for a certain distance, the possibility of several intersection points, i.e. of several states of equilibrium of the same market at different prices, obviously exists.

In most cases, of course, only a very short segment of the theoretically possible supply and demand curves can in reality exist, since greater price fluctuations do not often occur because of other possibilities of purchasing and selling.

When the proportions of exchange of *three* or several (*m*) commodities are to be found, we obviously have to consider the total supply and the total demand of each commodity as functions of *all* proportions of exchange or prices of the commodities concerned. The equalization of the supply and demand of each separate commodity supplies m equations,[1] amongst which, however, only $m - 1$ are independent. The variable prices are here also $m - 1$ in number in that, for instance, one of the commodities itself is taken as the standard of value.[2]

A geometrical interpretation is, of course, excluded here. At best, if it is a question of only three commodities, we could speak of supply and demand *surfaces*, if the quantities of goods concerned, together with the two prices or proportions of exchange of the three commodities, are drawn as co-ordinates in three dimensions.

These indications may suffice to show that the conventional teaching of supply and demand, by means of the marginal utility theory, seems to be capable of considerable extension and deepening. It is true that one is very soon confronted thereby with an almost hopeless entanglement of interacting economic relationships; but if the exact mode of treatment can do nothing else, it will at least be able to distinguish sharply between that which we know or are able to penetrate, and that about which we know, or can know, really nothing at all; and this is, after all, the beginning of all true science.

8—The law of costs. Walras's theory of production

So far we have only looked at the imaginary case where the valuation, on the part of each of the possessors, of the goods to be exchanged depends *solely* on the size of the possessed stock and the quantity of the commodity in question obtained by exchange, or, if two or several kinds of goods can partly replace each other, on all of these quantities of goods. This case includes, in reality, perhaps, the daily changes of market prices, and even these only in so far as it is a matter of goods which are intended for immediate consumption. In every other case buyers as well as sellers will keep watch over the future supply and demand and over the possibilities of production and sale in future, by which the present prices must also be influenced. And more especially, if the average level of prices

---

[1] In the case of three commodities, these are identical with equations (9).

[2] In the case of three commodities the equations (7), with the help of the equations (8), may be considered solved in x, y, z, etc.; in which case the positive x's and y's are conceived as (individual) demands and the negative ones as supplies, etc. (the appropriate $+$ or $-$ sign must in this case, of course, be regarded as given by the nature of the task).

during a longer period, e.g. during one or several years, is uncertain, then the factors of production must be taken into consideration before everything else. It is not simply commodities that are exchanged, but products, and in the last instance the productive services themselves: labour, natural resources and the employment of capital.

But *has* a new element really come into our problem of exchange? One would be inclined to think that the productive services could be treated in exactly the same way as the commodities, according to the rules of the equality or proportionality of their marginal utility for the owners, i.e. in this case the workers, the land-owners and the capitalists. Indeed, we shall see at once how such a manner of treatment of the problem was attempted by L. Walras.

Whoever desires a certain number of commodities, in fact desires by implication a certain amount of the productive services which are necessary for the production of just these commodities; and he himself has in the end, as means of payment for the goods successively demanded and consumed by him, nothing else to offer but the productive services of which he for his part can dispose, i.e. his labour in any case, then perhaps also the use of landed property or capital which he possesses. It could therefore seem as if the production and the exchange of goods were nothing else but an indirect exchange of the productive services concerned against each other, quite in accordance with the usual rules of the market; and this, moreover, was frequently asserted.

But the matter is certainly not as simple as this. Here the well-known dictum of J. S. Mill (to which he himself, to be sure, gave quite an undue extension) is confirmed, that 'demand for commodities is *not* demand for labour' (or for the other productive services). Production requires *time*, and the sellers of the productive services will generally not be able or willing to await the completion of the commodities in order to secure their remuneration from the amount realized by the sale: they obtain this remuneration from the proceeds of the production periods already completed. Production will therefore, in reality, never be like the simple market; it consists rather of a series of acts of exchange performed at different times which together span the whole period from the beginning of the production to the sale of the commodity in question. Only if one takes this fact into consideration can one adequately explain to oneself the role of capital in production, that mysterious 'productivity' of capital, and obtain at the same time the main key to the phenomenon of capital interest.[1] We shall discuss these questions in detail in the next chapter, where it will be our task to comment on the outstanding work done by Böhm-Bawerk. But first let us say something about the so-called law of costs in its older and newer forms.

Classical political economy had, as everybody knows, two ways of explaining exchange values: firstly, by pointing to the relationship between supply and demand—which, however, necessarily proved a little superficial without the inclusion of the concept of marginal utility; and secondly, by asserting that, at least on the home market, the exchange values of goods must finally always coincide with the cost of production. If the profits of the different entrepreneurs are included in the costs, this is certainly self-evident. But in order to be more than a mere triviality, and in order not to move in a hopeless circle, this mode of explanation had to seek for independent reasons for the different elements in costs. We have already seen how Ricardo's sagacity was able to give this really impossible task at least a formal solution. The element of cost, labour, was determined by the means of subsistence of workers, which was assumed to be approximately constant; rent was eliminated in the known manner; interest, finally, though it could not be determined *a priori*, was at least represented as a magnitude which is proportional to the magnitude of the capital advanced, or, which was assumed to be the same, to the amount of labour employed.

The modern theory of value could, of course, not approve of this mode of explanation. It noticed at once that the value of the elements of costs is determined in the last resort by nothing else but the value of the goods produced; so that value and costs must always be regarded as magnitudes dependent *on each other*. To my knowledge, only Leon Walras attempted successfully to do justice to these reciprocal relations and thus actually to lay down 'the equations of production.'

Walras sets out from the assumption that the real profit of enterprise is cancelled out by the reciprocal competition of

---

1 Even the exchange of finished goods requires time. In so far as it does this, it can be added to the production and is itself a source of capital interest.

entrepreneurs. Thus they are simply compensated for their work of managing the enterprise as other workers are, according to a measure fixed by competition. But then the assumption is made, or rather the *fiction* is introduced—and in this lies the weak point in Walras's presentation—that the entrepreneurs would buy 'on the market of the productive services' the services needed for their production of goods, namely the use of land, the various uses of capital,[1] and finally labour—but not against cash or commodities but simply against the promise to repay the same quantities of these services later after the conclusion of the production. But instead of really doing this, they would sell 'on the market of the products' the finished goods to those who offer the productive services and who appear now as consumers and, consequently, as buyers. In this way the entrepreneurs would be absolved from their promise to return the productive services as such; because the exchange value of the products must be equal to the productive services necessary for their production, if equilibrium between production and consumption is to exist and if the entrepreneurs are to have neither loss nor profit. The productive services themselves, therefore, are here exchanged against each other 'en fin de compte,' as Walras explicitly remarks, and this according to the principle of marginal utility; since the existing productive services possess a certain utility and marginal utility—directly for the owners themselves, as well as indirectly, in the form of finished products, for the consumers of these products (who on their part have also to dispose of productive services).

However ingenious this concept—developed by Walras in a strictly mathematical form—may appear, it nevertheless suffers from a fundamental mistake, which must necessarily render the result illusory. And this mistake is to have completely overlooked the significance of time in production. Although the productive services are measured by Walras according to units of time—so many years of lease, so many working days, etc.— in his presentation of the matter, the use, for instance, of one hectare of land for one year could be paid for in such a way that the owners of the land would be allowed at some future date to use a similar hectare of land for one year; and the same is true with regard to labour. This is obviously *not* the case.

[1] We shall soon see what is meant by these according to Walras.

It is also untrue that the owners of land are remunerated by the proceeds from the products made with their assistance— still less the workers; rather, they get their payment in *advance*. If this were not so, one could 'en fin de compte' completely overlook the part of capital in production—for the different parts of capital, machines, buildings, etc., are in the last instance products of labour and forces of nature—so that the production would finally have to be regarded as being completely without capital.

This mistake of Walras is connected with the peculiar interpretation of the concept of capital, to which we shall come back in the next chapter. He wants only durable goods, as, for instance, buildings and machines, to be considered as capital; on the other hand, consumable goods, as 'revenues,' he wants to put on a par with capital expenditure. What Adam Smith called circulating capital, raw materials, half-finished goods, etc., as well as the means of subsistence of workers and of other persons employed in the production, are, according to Walras, *revenues*, and bear no interest themselves (though they can be used for the production of new interest-bearing parts of capital). This is, of course, not correct. However the scientific terminology is arranged, the actual facts cannot be altered. Consumable goods certainly bear interest, if they are used for production or otherwise as capital; and the fact that they do this is just the main problem of the theory of capital interest.

At this point, therefore, we are led directly towards a thorough investigation into the nature of capital interest, to which we shall now proceed.

II

The New Theory of Capital

AND ITS RELATIONS TO THE THEORY OF WAGES,
GROUND-RENT AND VALUES OF GOODS[1]

1—The concept of capital

It is difficult, if not impossible, to define the concept of capital
in a wholly satisfactory way, that is to say, in a way which
would combine scientific precision with close adherence to
everyday language. In the exact sciences one simply disregards
the ordinary use of the language and creates an entirely new
terminology; but this is not yet possible in a subject like political
economy, which is and must be wholly concerned with practical
problems. Considerably more harm than advantage would
result from it.

But when we think of the history of the development of the
concept of capital it is easy to understand why, in everyday
life, the use of language became so very vague just at this point.
Originally the word expressed, as we know, simply the main
stock of a loan (*capitale* or *capitalis pars debiti*) as contrasted
with the interest, and therefore an interest-bearing sum of
money. All further meanings of the word are now obtained by
more or less apt extensions of this root concept.

It was most natural to wish to apply the name capital to *all*
interest-bearing objects of wealth—*that is to say, all goods or
groups of goods which procure for their possessors an income,
without being consumed themselves in this process*; and all the
more so, in that all sources of income excepting human abilities
themselves obtained a money or capital value with the increasing
money circulation.

On the other hand, I do not think it permissible to say, with
Böhm-Bawerk,[2] that the other interest-bearing goods received

---

[1] Throughout this chapter I shall use as fundamental the excellent works of
Böhm-Bawerk, especially his *Positive Theorie des Kapitals*, which, I may be
allowed to assume, is known to most readers.

[2] *Positive Theorie des Kapitals*, p. 24.

the name capital because it 'had become clear that the interest-bearing power of sterile money was, after all, a borrowed one—borrowed from the fruitful power of objects which could be bought for money.' This was indeed a popular way of explaining the origin of money interest; but if it had been really understood 'clearly,' then, properly speaking, money would have had to be excluded from the concept of capital.

But this Böhm-Bawerk himself does not do, and he is right; for the interest-bearing power of money is by no means a 'borrowed' one. When, for instance, money serves as a medium of exchange, it really creates the value or increase in value which is later added to it as interest—and even more. It is, however, true that so-called money capital is often money only in name; in reality it merely denotes a sum of goods estimated in money.

This extension of the concept of capital, through which it comes to mean approximately fortune or at least interest-bearing fortune, may be fittingly employed in several respects. It is usually adopted in socialist and other popular writings, so that in these writings capitalists and workers are more or less the same as propertied and unpropertied classes. The 'capital market,' in the usual sense of the word, is made up, as we know, of all possible securities which represent interest-bearing fortune.

For most economic considerations, however, a certain limitation of this more general concept proved expedient. A concrete sum of money has obviously its analogue and counterpart not so much in landed property or other natural sources of goods as in the produced goods themselves; it is a type of *stored-up* wealth. The most important economic difference between landed property and produced goods seems to lie in the fact that the former yields its useful services only successively in a chronological sequence previously determined and unchangeable, but, to compensate for this, in an infinite sequence. Produced goods, on the other hand, can yield only a finite number of useful services, but in an almost optional sequence, much as a sum of money can be spent either all at once or by instalments over a longer period. This distinction, however, is not precise. An ore-mine or coal-pit, for instance, which can be exhausted at very different rates, has, from this point of view, more in common with a produced store of food or clothes than with landed property agriculturally used. On the other hand, a dwelling-house, for instance, which lasts perhaps for centuries, but which can provide accommodation for only a certain number of people at one and the same time, has, from the economic point of view, very much in common with landed property. However, the above-mentioned attribute of most produced goods is important, especially with regard to further production: it can be said of the tools of production that the more they can be used optionally the more they preserve a capitalistic character (in its narrower sense); for instance, machines, which can be made to run quicker or slower, or can stop, without suffering wear and tear, etc. Other arrangements, on the contrary—for instance, certain land improvements—once carried through, become so completely part and parcel of the landed property that they lose the above-mentioned character; that is to say, they are now really rent-goods and no longer capital-goods in the narrower sense of the phrase.

The seemingly paradoxical phenomenon, that consumable goods—that is to say, goods which exhaust or seem to exhaust their whole content of usefulness in a limited series of acts of use—can nevertheless be employed 'capitalistically,' so that their entire value remains stored up for the owner, and yet provides him with an income—this *perpetuum mobile* of the economic mechanism forms, as was said previously, the real pith of the theory of capital, which we shall now consider more closely.[1]

On the whole, of course, this can only happen through the re-creation by production (in the widest sense of the word, which includes traffic) of the consumable goods or their equivalent in value. Their former existence must, in this case, be a necessary condition of the production, otherwise a part of the produced goods could not possibly fall to the owner of the capital as *owner*.

But according to the usual conception, other means of acquisition are supposed to exist besides production (in the above-mentioned widest sense), and accordingly a further

---

[1] Inversion of this seeming paradox produces the question, How is it that goods which can yield, according to their nature, an infinite number of useful services, above all landed property, possess nevertheless only a finite capital value?

distinction should be made between '*private* capital' and
'*national* capital'—or as it ought to be called, according to
Böhm-Bawerk, '*social* capital'—where the former category
comprises all *means of acquisition* (usually with the exception of
landed property), whilst the latter comprises only the real
means of production.

I am doubtful whether this distinction is really a scientifically
fruitful one. It is, of course, allowable in this as well as in
other economic spheres to keep the point of view of private
enterprise separate from the social point of view. But I think
there is little justification for the attempt to draw up certain
categories of goods, some of which are supposed to be capital
only from the point of view of private enterprise, whilst others
are supposed to be capital from the social point of view as well.

In Böhm-Bawerk's opinion, dwelling-houses, for instance,
can only represent private capital (if they are let to others)—
not social capital, because they are only consumption goods,
not productive goods. It is true that they yield their useful
services spontaneously, without considerable addition of labour.
But the same is true to a large extent of meadows, woods,
preserves, etc., which, however, cannot be denied the name of
capital—in the 'social' sense of the word—if one wants to extend
this concept to landed property at all. Therefore it seems best
to me to put dwelling-houses in the same category as landed
property. However, if they are to be regarded as capital at all,
it seems clear to me that they must be considered as belonging
to social capital.

This would indeed still be contrary to the remark of Adam
Smith quoted by Böhm-Bawerk, that the community (as
contrasted with a single individual) 'can only enrich itself by
production.' But the *enrichment* of the community is a matter
of comparative detail. Nor, by the way, is the private capitalist
primarily *enriched* by interest, but lives on it. The chief aim of
economic life, for the community as well as for the individual,
is obviously to maintain the level of well-being already achieved.
And this end is served not only by real production, but by
the mere storing-up of durable utility goods regardless
of whether these are produced or were the direct gift of
Nature. The opinion that durable goods cease to be capital
the moment they are consumed by their owner and consequently
no longer provide him with a money income, is, as A. Marshall

remarks,[1] really nothing but a relic of the prejudices of the old mercantile system.

It is not quite clear to me in what way exactly the poor *circulating libraries* have offended, which, along with articles for hire (e.g. *fancy-dresses* and the like), must serve as standing examples of things which represent only private, but not social capital. As long as social conditions do not make it possible for everybody to possess an extensive collection of books, public libraries, whether they can be used free of charge or for a fee, are certainly an ingredient, and a not unimportant one, in social capital. The keeping of a lending library is a business, like all the others. If now, with Böhm-Bawerk—and quite correctly, as I see it—one calls 'the consumption goods in the hands of producers and merchants, stored up as warehouse stock,' capital and, what is more, *social* capital,[2] then it seems strangely inconsistent to wish to exclude lending libraries simply because it is their purpose to sell reading-matter instead of books.

But more important is the question of what is to be done with the 'means of subsistence of workers.' Strange to say, Böhm-Bawerk saw that he was obliged to place this important category of goods called by Jevons, as is well known, the real substance of productive and consequently of social capital, in the mixed collection of exclusively private capital together with 'rentable houses and lending libraries.' For to this collection belong, according to him, 'all those consumption goods which their owner does not use himself but employs by exchange (selling, letting, lending) for the acquisition of other goods'; and amongst them must be included, as he explicitly remarks, the 'means of subsistence which the entrepreneurs advance to their workers.'[3]

But again: he himself, a few pages before, has represented the 'stored-up consumption goods in the hands of producers and merchants' as social capital, and to money he gives the

---

[1] *Principles of Economics*, p. 124. Adam Smith's remark (*Wealth of Nations*, vol. II, chapter I), that houses let to a tenant and similar goods can only be reckoned as private capital for the simple reason that rent must always be taken from any *other* source of income, is meaningless. The same is, after all, true of *every* money income and, generally speaking, of every income which arises from *exchange*. If a craftsman or a business-man reckons his landlord as customer, his income is drawn from the landlord's, just as the landlord's is drawn from his.

[2] Op. cit., p. 70.   [3] Op. cit., p. 76.

same name. If now wages, as usual, are paid in money and the workers themselves obtain what they require from the merchants, then these goods, before they pass into the hands of the workers, are social capital according to Böhm-Bawerk's terminology. But if the entrepreneur buys the same goods for the same money, in order to transfer them subsequently as wages to the workers, then these goods in the hands of the entrepreneurs—and once again before they pass to the workers—would not be social capital any longer, but simply private capital!

That a writer so sagacious and circumspect as Böhm-Bawerk could be led to such strange conclusions, is, if I am not mistaken, due to a circumstance which, in other respects as well, has done great damage in political economy, namely to the vague idea that from the *economic* point of view it is, practically speaking, of no consequence to whom the goods belong, provided only they are there. As soon as it is a question of deciding whether or not the means of subsistence of workers are social capital, Böhm-Bawerk always reasons as if these means of subsistence were *already* in the hands of the workers. But since workers are human beings and members of the community—at least according to the modern way of thinking—their means of subsistence must be regarded in the same way as those of the rest of the population. 'The goods with which the working members of the community feed, warm and clothe themselves, are goods for immediate consumption, not means of production.'[1]

Economically understood, this is certainly true. It could even be added that these goods, from the technical point of view also, are means of production only in so far as they are really converted into labour, so that only that portion of the means of subsistence which corresponds to about the exact minimum of life would, in fact, (technically) be productive. From the economic point of view, the means of subsistence, *as soon as they have passed into the possession of the workers*, are no longer means of production at all and no longer capital (either 'social' or 'private'), because *their productive equivalent* has in this case already been parted with and has entered *into the possession of the capitalist*.

But if the means of subsistence have not yet passed over into

1 Böhm-Bawerk, op. cit., p. 73.

the hands of the workers, but are still (directly or indirectly through money) in the possession of the capitalist, then they are undoubtedly means of production, *because they serve for the purchase of labour*.[1]

It will perhaps be best, if we are to find our way in this rather complicated state of affairs, to base our thinking throughout upon the assumption of a *stationary community*, as the simplest hypothesis. For all productive factors, and consequently capital too, could then be considered as approximately *constant* magnitudes. Though in this case the forms of the latter change, its total value remains unchanged, since in place of the consumed capital goods new ones of equivalent value enter successively.

But Böhm-Bawerk goes on to remark that if the whole national subsistence fund is called capital, 'then not only must the means of subsistence of the productive workers be reckoned as capital, but also the subsistence of the capitalists and land-owners, as standing in exactly the same indirect relation to the adoption of capitalist methods of production.'[2] As far as the landowners are concerned, this is undoubtedly correct. The landowners, too, live during production, which in certain cases takes several years before the products are finished; that is to say, they live on their ground-rents. Therefore, either they are capitalists themselves (at least up to the amount of the ground-rents due after the completion of the production process), or they get their 'subsistence,' that is to say their rents, as an advance from the capitalists, who must in consequence successively keep in stock the consumption goods concerned or the money for them. And in so far as these consumption goods in the hands of the capitalists serve for the purchase of the productive services of land, they must certainly be conceived as productive capital. But if they have passed into the possession of the landowners, they no longer serve production and are therefore no longer capital; but then their equivalent, the services of the land, raw materials, etc., is already added to the capital stock of the country.

Lastly, so far as the means of subsistence of capitalists themselves are concerned, one might be tempted to give up calling these capital, and to call them instead just—*interest*.

---

[1] It must not be overlooked that the role of the capitalist and that of the worker can also be united in *one and the same person*.

[2] Op. cit., p. 75.

Consistency requires, however, that they should be thought of all the time as capital until the moment when they find themselves in the possession of the *consumers* concerned. In other words, capital is regarded in stationary economy as capable of a certain, but on the whole not noticeable, oscillation, since it continuously increases by interest and is in the same way continuously decreased by the consumption of this interest.

The distinction between private and social capital laid down by Adam Smith and even extended by Böhm-Bawerk, does not therefore really exist, in my opinion. Social capital simply consists of the sum of private capitals. One might think that at least in one point a real difference must be made between social and private capital, namely in respect of the *consumption loan*. But this difficulty disappears at once if, according to the commendable example of Böhm-Bawerk, we reckon as capital only *material goods*, but not either 'rights and situations' (*Rechte und Verhältnisse*) or personal attributes. A patrimony, dissipated by the heir in advance of his inheriting it, who thus gets into debt, exists afterwards solely in the form of a *claim*, which at the moment is not counterbalanced by a single material commodity and the like is true of every consumption loan.

But claims *can*, of course, be reckoned as belonging to capital (as social capital, to be sure), if at the same time debts are admitted into the final sum of social capital as *negative* items or quantities.

It must, however, be remarked that social capital, so carefully defined by Böhm-Bawerk, plays almost no part in his following investigations. When he speaks about the real problems of the theory of capital interest, the difference, so laboriously demonstrated, between 'aggregate of the intermediate products' (social capital) and 'national subsistence fund' (also called by him 'national capital') is again missing. And rightly so; for if the sphere of 'intermediate products' is extended over the entire domain of production in its widest sense, up to the moment of consumption,[1] all concepts are, in fact, simply congruent:

[1] We say intentionally, 'up to the moment of consumption'; for it is after all of little importance whether the duration of life of capital is or is not theoretically prolonged by several hours, days or even weeks. The economic sign that goods cease to be capital-goods is, as I see it, this—that they, so to speak, have passed into the *lawful* possession of the consumers; that is to say, are exchanged for some capitalistic equivalent: labour, the use of land, other capital-goods or

social or productive capital, national subsistence fund or 'national capital,' and finally private capital or simply capital (with the exception of landed property).

To sum up: in the wider sense, *all* interest-bearing (material) goods are capital; but the different capitals do not all play the same economic role. There is 'capital in the narrower sense,' as distinct from 'capital in the wider sense.' But it is more difficult to decide *where* the line of demarcation can best be drawn here—whether, as is usually assumed, it ought simply to separate produced goods from pure natural goods (landed property), or (according to Wieser) must be more closely related to the 'consumability and mobility,' and therefore the ready availability and utilization of capital-goods in the narrower sense.

Probably, too, the different economic problems will require a different delimitation of the concept, just as in popular terminology the word capital forms a real Proteus concept.

However, it seems best to me for the purposes of the following investigation to class the different capitals simply *according to their durability*. In what follows I shall call the highly durable goods rent-goods, whether they are products themselves, or, like virgin soil, goods furnished by nature itself and whether they yield useful services spontaneously or only by the addition of human labour.[1] Consumable or quickly exhausted production or consumption goods, so long as the latter are not yet in the hands of consumers, I shall call capital-goods or capital in the narrower sense.[2]

The boundary line in this case remains to be determined, of course. However, this indeterminateness is of no importance

money. Nevertheless, the consumers—or the persons so named by us for the sake of simplicity—*can* in this case partly deny themselves the consumption goods which now belong to them lawfully and use them as *new* capital-goods. We have already dealt with the position of durable consumption goods.

[1] According to Böhm-Bawerk the productive undertakings designed to improve landed property in so far as they preserve an independent character and do not become completely absorbed in the landed property (e.g. dams, pipes, etc.), ought to be called capital. But of what importance is this independent character here? When it is a question of the level of interest or wages, these goods have exactly the same importance as landed property itself, provided only they are sufficiently durable.

[2] Money has in this case a remarkable double position. For the community as a whole it is a rent-commodity; what is more, rent (the utility of money) received by the community is many times in excess of the amount of the usual money interest. For the single possessor it is a capital-good.

when it is merely a question of explaining the nature of capital interest. On the other hand, as soon as one approaches the problem of ascertaining exactly the reasons which determine the level of interest and the relations between capital-interest, wages and ground-rent (the imputation of the productive factors, according to Wieser's terminology), it at once appears necessary to unite the different capital-goods, as far as possible, in one *sum*; which, of course, assumes a previous, more or less rigorous, demarcation of the sphere of capital. This obviously cannot be done with this or that *definition* established *a priori*; on the contrary, it requires an exact exploration of the true functions of these economic forces and also an investigation into how far these forces can really be united in one sum or—to use an analogy from mechanics—in one single *resultant*. This sum or resultant would then be the capital—within the limits of the problem concerned.

If we wish to interpret the divergent views regarding the concept of capital as a *testimonium paupertatis* of political economy, we shall not be wholly wrong. Only it must be remembered that strict definitions of concepts always form the keystone rather than the basis of a scientific system; and it will be a comfort to reflect that even the most exact of the sciences, mathematics, has not yet arrived at satisfactory definitions.

2—Böhm-Bawerk's theory of interest and the earlier theories

How does interest arise, and in particular, how can consumable goods bear interest; that is to say, at least in appearance yield useful services, without thereby diminishing in value?

I should like to let Böhm-Bawerk speak on this question. No one can have read his two volumes *Kapital und Kapitalzins* carefully without having gained therefrom a real enrichment of his theoretical knowledge. If we cannot agree with all his conclusions, yet we must gratefully acknowledge that scarcely any other author has penetrated so deeply as he into the real nature of the matter. At any rate, no one has been able to combine profundity and clarity to the extent that he has done.

His one fault, it seems to me, is that he sometimes wants to be too profound. He loves to pile up theoretical difficulties, in order, of course, to remove them later on—for the most part satisfactorily, but in a way which is somewhat confusing to the ordinary reader.

The simple formula in which Böhm-Bawerk wishes to comprehend all phenomena in the realm of capital interest, and by which all earlier theories of interest are to be replaced, runs, as is well known, as follows: *Interest is an agio which comes into being when present and future goods are exchanged.* It rests solely on the *relationship between present and future in human economy* and simply expresses the fact that *present goods* (at least according to the contemporary valuation) *are as a rule more valuable than future goods of the same kind and number.*

There can be no doubt that this formula governs the problem of interest in its whole extent[1]—and it is no mere tautology, which simply expresses that $A = A$, interest is—interest! The clarifying element, newly added, lies in the word *exchange*: the problem of interest can now be treated as a true problem of exchange. In particular, the consideration of marginal utility will play the same part in the theory of interest as in the theory of ordinary exchange. And this applies to 'natural interest' as well as to interest on loans. He who parts with present goods, in order in some way or other to obtain future goods of the same kind, really makes an exchange between two uses of the same commodity. He thus performs the very action which we, at the beginning of our remarks concerning exchange, put forward as its simplest form; and the degree in which he does this is regulated, as there, by the proportion of *two marginal utilities* (that of the present goods and that of the future goods, according to the contemporary valuation).

Also, the interest on the loan, just like the exchange value in the case of ordinary exchange, will depend on *two proportions of marginal utility*; that is to say, it will depend first on the proportion between the marginal utility of present and that of future goods *for the creditor*, and secondly on the proportion between the analogous marginal utilities *for the debtor*. Usually in this case the marginal utility of present goods for *both* will prove to be higher than the marginal utility of future goods of *the same* kind and *number*; so that the interest almost always

---

[1] It is, in my opinion, even more comprehensive than the problem itself, in that it also includes interest phenomena where no interest-bearing capital exists any longer (as in the case of a consumption loan).

turns out to be *positive*—that is to say, it will be paid by the debtor. The proportion of marginal utility can finally become *identical* on both sides, but not the *proportion of the total utility*. This, on the contrary, must always be different, if a loan is to take place at all, and in such a way that the debtor as opposed to the creditor always values present goods relatively higher. The interest which must really be paid will then fall somewhere or other between these two different valuations.[1]

The passages in which he discusses how and why present goods, according to the existing valuation, almost always possess a higher utility or marginal utility respectively than future goods, belong to the best-known and most important parts of Böhm-Bawerk's book. These we shall now examine briefly.

The first main ground is stated to be *the difference in the circumstances of want and provision at different periods of time.*

Whether this can rightly be conceived as a *main* ground of the phenomenon of interest, is open to question. In a stationary economy (which in my opinion must always be considered first as the simplest case), needs and their satisfaction are to be understood as, on an average, constant magnitudes. In such an economy also, it is true, several persons, or whole age-groups, could expect a more abundant satisfaction in the future than now. But besides these there are other individuals for whom the opposite is true; so that it seems as if, under this assumption, supply of, and demand for, present goods against future goods must equal each other also at *par*.

Böhm-Bawerk remarks, however, that even where provision for the future will presumably be *less plentiful*, the present goods must at least be equal in value to the future goods, since they can, if necessary, easily be preserved for use in the future. This is certainly a great exaggeration. Böhm-Bawerk mentions, to be sure, 'an exception' to this rule—in respect, that is, of 'perishable goods, such as ice, fruit, and so forth.' But this applies in a greater or less degree to all food-stuffs without exception. Why, there are perhaps *no* goods apart from precious metals or stones, for instance, whose preservation for the future does not require

[1] In his book *Principii di economia pura* (p. 301), M. Pantaleoni opposes Böhm-Bawerk in saying that, if it were true that a present commodity possessed a higher marginal utility than a future commodity, the loan would in fact be a purposeless transaction, because like would merely be exchanged against like. The superficiality of this objection is obvious after what has been said above.

special care and effort, with the additional risk that they may yet be lost in a fire or by some such misfortune.[1]

In countries with a great future before them, like certain colonial countries, more plentiful provision for the future can admittedly be regarded as a common fact, and undoubtedly contributes to the level of the rate of interest customary there. In countries with a long-established culture, and in the case of a practically stationary economy, the higher valuation of present as against future goods will, on the other hand—if the possibility of a productive application of these is disregarded—occur to a much more limited extent than Böhm-Bawerk seems to think.

However, this would have been the place to discuss a circumstance which Böhm-Bawerk only mentions later in another connexion and only in passing—namely, that the use of present goods for the future, under otherwise similar circumstances, must *in itself* call forth for the possessor in question a more plentiful provision for the future as distinct from the present, and therefore, in its turn, lead to the higher valuation of present goods.

It is just this circumstance which, in combination with the second main ground, soon to be mentioned, sets bounds to the sacrifice of present pleasures in the interests of the future; that is to say, *the formation of capital.*

Böhm-Bawerk's *second main ground*—the subjective and often *incorrect* underestimation of future wants resulting from defects of imagination or will—is without doubt of the utmost importance. Not only does it constitute, in combination with the uncertainty of all legal and economic affairs, the chief cause of the feeble formation of capital and the excessively high rate of interest in all primitive economies, but scarcely a day goes by without its effects being traced by each one of us to some extent.

But when Böhm-Bawerk mentions in this connexion the 'consideration of the shortness and uncertainty of our life,' and asserts: 'Payments which become due in 100, 50 or even only 20 years lose value for all . . . receivers in view of the uncertainty of their expectation of life,' it seems to me open to

---

[1] If this were not the case, one would hear little of times of famine and distress, and so on. Nothing seems easier than to do as Joseph and Pharaoh did and, when the harvest is good, put aside the surplus for use when the harvest is bad. But the practical solution of this problem soon proves to be a very difficult one, not only because of the improvidence of individuals, but first and foremost because of the cost and inconvenience of the storage itself.

question whether one can speak here only of *subjective* under-estimation. Our children, grandchildren and great-grand-children will in general have at their disposal the same means of satisfying their needs as we. Whether we, by denying our-selves now, can give them a *corresponding* advantage, therefore remains doubtful, especially with regard to the more distant generations of our posterity, whose well-being will depend only to a very limited extent on us. We will not allow ourselves to be held up by this, however, but proceed now to the *third* and last of the *main grounds* put forward by Böhm-Bawerk.

This, as the author himself admits, is practically identical with what in former times one used to understand by the phrase 'productivity of capital.' Since, however, as is well known, he cannot recognize the 'productivity theory' as relevant, he now endeavours to explain independently why present goods are, 'as a rule, on technical grounds, preferable instruments for the satisfaction of our needs and assure us, therefore, of a higher marginal utility' than future goods.

According to him the explanation lies in the fact '*that time-consuming, round-about methods of production are more pro-ductive. That is to say, given the same quantity of means of production, the lengthier the productive method employed, the greater the quantity of products that can be obtained.*' The role of capital in production is therefore, as was already emphasized by Jevons, simply this, that it can introduce a shorter or longer interval of time between the beginning and the completion of production, whereas primitive production, carried on without capital, must always live 'from hand to mouth.'

With a certain sum of primary productive forces—for instance, with one working month which is to-day at our disposal—we shall be able to produce more goods if it is used as the starting-point of a period of production of one year, than if we were to use it for the immediate production of goods of the same kind; and consequently more goods also than could be obtained if one of next year's working months were used to produce goods straight away. If even lengthier methods of production are adopted, so that, for instance, the goods in question are intended to be ready in two years' time, the superiority of to-day's working month over next year's working month holds good also; for the former could then be employed as the starting-point of a *two*-year production process, whilst the latter could at best be employed as the starting-point of a *one*-year production process, and so on. In so far as the above-mentioned fact can be supposed to be generally applicable, the technical superiority of present productive forces (labour or natural forces) over future ones is proved.

This theory is, however, somewhat more amply constructed than the older productivity theory (Thünen's), which simply refers to the fact that by sacrificing, for instance, a hundred present units of goods, the future production *can be increased by more* than a hundred units of goods of the same kind.[1] Fundamentally, however, both theories are identical, and the agreement even becomes complete when Böhm-Bawerk arrives at the question: Why have present *consumption goods*, too, an advantage over future consumption goods?

Here, too, Böhm-Bawerk tries to formulate his explanation slightly differently. He says (*Positive Theorie*, p. 287): 'Command over a sum of present consumption goods provides us with the means of subsistence during the current economic period. This leaves the means of production which we have at our disposal for just this period (labour, uses of land, capital-goods) free for the technically more productive service of the future, and gives us the more·abundant product attainable by them in longer methods of production. On the other hand, of course, command over a sum of future consumption goods leaves the present unprovided for, and consequently leaves us under the necessity of directing the means of production that are at our command now, wholly or partially to the service of the present. But this involves curtailment of the production process and a correspondingly diminished product. The difference in the two products is the advantage associated with the possession of present consumption goods.'

But this is immediately clear only when it is a question of the production of consumption goods of *precisely the same kind* as

---

[1] Here, obviously, we are speaking only of the well-thought-out and 'motivated' productivity theory of a writer like Thünen. Böhm-Bawerk has a much easier task with most of the other so-called productivity theorists, who were often not even able to distinguish between product of capital and interest on capital. I shall not even mention the incredible superficialities of a writer like Carey. Böhm-Bawerk rightly says of this author, that 'his theory belongs to those which not only discredit their author, but also the study which is betrayed into accepting them so faithfully; and this not because of its errors, but because of the unpardonable nature of the mistakes by which it errs.' (*Kritik und Geschichte der Kapitalzinstheorie*, p. 179.)

the ones at our disposal. Otherwise it will always be open to doubt whether, just because of the more abundant future production of the goods (*A*) in question, their value, as compared with the value of the consumption goods (*B*) available *before*, will not be so greatly diminished that finally it will be of no consequence whether this sum of (*B*) is available now or in future. This difficulty vanishes when it is merely a question of the production of consumption goods of the same kind—but here we find ourselves in the very midst of Thünen's productivity theory.

Böhm-Bawerk himself, however, did not, or could not, remove the objection which he directed against this theory in the first volume of his book—namely, that it explains at best the *physical*, but not the *value* production of capital. For the demand which he there makes of the productivity theorists was, after all, not to explain why present goods are higher in value than future goods of the same number and kind *according to the present valuation*—this (in so far as the above-mentioned fact is generally true) Thünen's theory certainly explains as well as his own theory, though in a somewhat more concise manner—but *why the product of capital, when it becomes due, should be more valuable than the sacrificed capital commodity itself.* But Böhm-Bawerk has not explained this either; and it can after all only be explained *if one sets out from the assumption of a nearly stationary position of economy.*

Nor has Böhm-Bawerk answered, by his explanation set forth above, his further main objection to the productivity theory: Are the surplus values or surplus products obtained by the use of capital really added to the capital itself, or do they perhaps fall to the share of the other contributing factors of production, labour, landed property, etc.? It may be true that more future products can be produced with a present working month than with a next year's working month. But will this surplus benefit the possessor of to-day's working month without more ado? That is not clear in itself (for nothing can be produced at all with working-time alone and without the use of the forces of nature). It is also not generally true, because the share which belongs to the different factors of production depends entirely on the position of the market. This no one has shown more clearly and finely than Böhm-Bawerk himself in the later parts of his work.

But in the discussion of this problem one is always obliged to assume an approximately stationary economy as the simplest and fundamental case, and as soon as this assumption is made, his objections to Thünen's theory answer themselves.

Another question which requires to be answered is why this stationary condition, or what comes to about the same thing *here*, a society in which there is only a slow progression, can be assumed as a rule in theory as well as in practice, and why the incomes of capitalists, landowners and workers are on the whole consumed instead of being hoarded and added to the stock of capital. And although this question is closely connected with the problem of interest, it remains nevertheless a question in itself. In my opinion, Böhm-Bawerk must be blamed for having mixed up the two questions of the origin of interest and the origin of interest-bearing capital itself—in his criticism of the older theories of interest as well as in his own positive presentation—instead of separating them in a truly scientific manner.

And finally a word ought to be said about the *Use theory*. As is well known, this theory sets out from interest on durable goods, conceiving interest as the price for the use of the commodity during a given time. If the commodity is subject to wear and tear, interest is conceived as the price of its *net* use; since trouble and labour, necessary for the replacement of the wear and tear which has taken place, are subtracted from the utility of the simple use of the commodity. Whether the value of the commodity remains unchanged in this case and whether the commodity really possesses a capital-value which could be compared with the value of the useful services themselves, remains unsettled.[1] It is merely assumed that the commodity keeps its *substance*, so that it can yield identical useful services in the future also. Once we have adopted this terminology, it is, in my opinion, no *fiction*, but a scientific *generalization*, if these concepts of use and net use respectively are extended to cover consumable goods as well. In the case of durable goods, too, it is, after all, of no consequence whether the wear and tear amounts to more or less, provided only they

---

1 The usual explanation of capital-value of durable, produced goods, such as a dwelling-house, by reference to the costs of production and reproduction, is, of course, unscientific and amounts to mixing up and lumping together cause and effect.

are replaced by continuous repairs. But then the wear and tear can, as in the case of consumable goods, finally extend to the whole commodity, provided its use includes the repair or reproduction of the commodity itself or of an identical commodity. If now this use consists precisely in the acquisition of goods of the same kind as the capital commodity concerned, then obviously a rate of *interest* is hereby already determined (an element in the determination of the average rate of interest), which can lead retrospectively to a higher estimate of the capital-value of durable goods.

This view can be regarded as more or less satisfactory and scientifically fruitful. To explain it as depending merely on *delusion* seems to me unjustified. And when Böhm-Bawerk[1] finds it ridiculous that the Use theory should presuppose the possibility of 'transferring to someone *a little more than the whole of something*, that is to say, transferring along with the possession of the loaned object, the right to each and every use which is to be got from the object until it is completely used up, plus a separate fragment of use for which interest can be separately demanded,' then the answer is simply, that interest is *not* demanded or given for some 'separate fragment of use' but in fact 'for every scrap of use which is to be got from the article'—use, that is to say, *which is only compatible with* the repair of the article itself or its replacement by an identical one.[2]

The mode of explanation of the Use theory (and of the productivity theory) is only excluded in the case of the pure consumption loan. This case is to be understood, rather, from

[1] *Positive Theorie des Kapitales*, p. 301.

[2] Particularly as regards the question of the 'use of money,' the Use theory can be applied with success. When we so apply it we are generally disturbed by the fact that a borrowed sum of money is 'used' by the debtor once only, and for the most part immediately after the receipt of the loan. In fact, however, he uses the money at least *twice*, once for the purchase, and once for the *sale* of goods; and in this case the circulation of the money which has taken place in the meantime generally enables him to sell the purchased commodity at a profit later on. This becomes especially clear if one looks at the simplest case where no real production is involved but the money *merely* serves for the exchange— that is to say, for the economically more advantageous distribution of the existing goods. If we assume that this sum constitutes the only money in circulation within the economy in question, then the situation which we have met before in the case of the exchange of several commodities arises, and we can follow *the identical moneys* right up to the time of the repayment of the loan. In this case at any rate, interest appears first not in the form of money but in the form of goods.

the point of view of an exchange between a present and a future commodity.[1]

Böhm-Bawerk's formula is thus undoubtedly the most general of all. It brings out better than the earlier explanations the true essence of the matter, namely the economic significance of *time*, and it adapts itself quite as well as any other mode of explanation to the different phenomena of interest. This formula consequently represents, in my opinion, an important scientific advance—more, however, in the sense that it supplies what was missing in the older explanations than in the sense that it substitutes for possibly false or meaningless ideas a completely new and altogether true interpretation, as, to be sure, Böhm-Bawerk himself on more than one occasion states.

3—The period of production. Capital-goods and 'rent-goods'

The main significance of Böhm-Bawerk's theory lies, however, in my opinion, in the masterly way in which the role of capital in production is discussed there. In the last analysis this role consists, as has already been said, simply and solely in making possible the introduction of a longer period of time between the beginning and the conclusion of the process of production of the commodity concerned and consequently the adoption of a more productive round-about method of production than would be possible if production were less strong in capital or totally devoid of capital. Consequently, free capital, by its very nature, consists of a sum of means of subsistence, i.e. consumption goods which are advanced to the workers and the owners of the forces of nature by the capitalists during production; that is to say, they are exchanged for labour and services of the land. This sum, however, need not, at any rate at the beginning of production, be kept available; it need only become realizable successively. *On an average*, however, it is consumed some time *before* the completion of the work (about half-way through the production). If now at any point of time we take, so to speak, a cross-section of the production, this labour which has been done in advance, and these stored-up

[1] Strictly speaking, however, as was indicated above, interest on a consumption loan does not belong to the sphere of true capital interest, since here the loaned 'capital' continues to exist not as a material commodity but merely as a claim and the repayment takes place by a *new* formation of capital on the part of the debtor (or by diminution of already existing capital).

services of the land, appear in the form of raw materials, tools, half-finished products, and so on, which represent fixed capital. They are an indication of the length of the period of production. In proportion as these and, consequently, the invested capital, are greater, the proportion of workers occupied in the final stage of production decreases. This smaller number, however, produces a larger quantity of finished goods than the larger number at work during a shorter period of production, and still more than the whole number of workers occupied in production for present use which is carried on without capital. The greater the amount of capital that can be used in the production, that is to say, the lengthier the average period of production that can be applied, the greater will be the annual production of finished consumption goods, provided the same number of workers and the same area of the country are involved.

This is not to say, of course, that *all* technical advances must necessarily lead to the lengthening of the production processes which were usual before. But in so far as they do *not* lead to this lengthening, they do not make necessary an increase in the existing capital (or only temporarily). Capital can even be freed in this process. They simply operate, therefore, as if human labour or Nature under otherwise unchanged circumstances had become more productive.

In most cases, however, technical advances will necessitate all kinds of preparatory work; they will lead, that is to say, to new round-about methods of production and so make necessary the formation of new capital. There can be no doubt that in our time an incomparably greater accumulation of capital has taken place than at any time in the past.[1]

Since, therefore, the relatively definite and very simple

[1] Adam Smith (*Wealth of Nations*, vol. II, Introduction) tried to explain the need for capital formation by the *division of labour*, since the latter can only come about if the subsistence of the workers concerned is already assured by the accumulation of a given supply of food. But this seems to me to be a false conclusion. Division of labour by itself does not lengthen the period of production, but shortens it, and therefore does not in fact make necessary new capital formation (but does make necessary a certain concentration of the already existing capital). On the other hand, however, as is well known, division of labour is one of the most powerful instruments of production: many round-about methods of production which would otherwise not be sufficiently remunerative, become so by division of labour; and to this extent, of course, the possibility of division of labour becomes indirectly an effectual cause of the adoption of these round-about methods and consequently of the accumulation of new capital.

concept of the lengthening of the process of production replaces the older, vague, and multiform idea of productivity of capital, the theory of capital-interest can be treated in as exact a fashion as the theory of ground-rent before. As I shall try to show later, both of these together constitute the elements which we shall need if we are to lay down the real factors which determine exchange value.

It is assumed in this case that within every single branch of business, the productivity of labour, for instance, the annual production of one worker, is, under otherwise constant circumstances, a *function* of the length of the production process— a function which increases with the length of this period but more slowly, so that the scale of the surplus returns becomes a decreasing one—an effect which entirely agrees with experience. Even if we assume that the length of the period of production and the productivity of production are continuously variable magnitudes, we shall still be in the sphere of reality. Sometimes, of course, there are inventions, due to which the method of production usual before is transformed so thoroughly that the length of the process as well as its productiveness becomes quite different. In most cases, however, production changes only gradually. The technical possibility of all kinds of 'improvements' is very often already present, but the economic possibility is still lacking: the new 'labour-saving' machines or processes were invented long ago, but their application is not yet profitable. It is only when an increase in wages or a decrease of capital-interest has taken place, or because of other reasons, that this application becomes just profitable enough to be adopted—a proof of the fact that in similar cases it is only a question of relatively *small* changes.[1]

Certain difficulties stand in the way of this interpretation, however. Some of these Böhm-Bawerk has removed, but not, in my opinion, all. The first is the division of labour which has the effect that, in reality, the whole process of production of any one commodity will practically never be completed by one and the same firm. This difficulty is, however, not one of principle. So long as it is only a question of average capital-interest, wages, etc., we can think of all these partial businesses,

---

[1] For several reasons, the constancy of these changes is still more evident if the average proportions within a certain branch of business, considered as a whole, are examined.

in so far as they contribute to the production of the same final product, as being united in one single business. But if we pursue this thought, it soon becomes clear that very often several different businesses meet in one and the same business, either retrospectively or in a future view, or, which is the same, one single business branches out into several. For instance, one and the same factory delivers machines which later will serve for the production of goods of various kinds. It will be difficult or even impossible always to determine exactly how much work, and especially how much labour done in advance, this or that machine has really cost. The average quantity of labour and period of production within each group can be found approximately only if the goods are here divided into larger groups.

Another difficulty is caused by the existence of *durable* (productive) goods. If these, like tools or machines, only last a few years, it will still be of some help to us that the work necessary to produce the machine is distributed to the goods produced by its aid. In this case the *average* life of the machine can be regarded as an indication of the average length of the period of production or as part of this. This expedient breaks down, however, when it is a question of production goods which last 50, 100 or more years. Böhm-Bawerk disregards this difficulty. He remarks[1]: 'A fraction of a working-day already expended hundreds of years ago, on account of its smallness, is in most cases of no importance.' But if with him we reckon amongst capital productive buildings, factories, store-houses, railways, etc., which are often very old, then, according to the above conception—after deduction of maintenance and running costs—the interest paid for the use of these capital-goods *must* necessarily be regarded as remuneration for a part of the work which has gone into their construction in these far-off times. Obviously, however, the original cost of construction no longer has any influence on the present-day level of rent of these buildings or on the freight charges of the railways in question; and if similar work is to be carried out to-day, its prospective returns in some distant future will have just as little significance for its present capital-value or profitableness[2]—as, by the way,

---

[1] Loc. cit., p. 95.

[2] Whether a capital-good, for example a dwelling-house, will presumably last only 50 or even 100 years, makes, on the assumption of a rate of interest of 5 per cent, a difference of not quite 9 per cent (8·72 per cent) to its present-day capital

Böhm-Bawerk himself explicitly emphasizes. In my opinion, however, it is precisely because of this that goods of greater durability (such as streets, railways, buildings, etc.) cannot be regarded or treated as capital in the narrower sense, but, once they are there, must be placed, economically speaking, in the same category as landed property itself. In other words, if, in accordance with Böhm-Bawerk's precedent which we ourselves shall later follow, all existing capitals are united in one sum, in order to use this sum as an element in the theoretical determination of the level of interest and of wages, it would be misleading to think of the capital value of all railways, buildings, etc., as being included in this sum. This value is rather, like the capital value of landed property itself, to be thought of as a secondary phenomenon which has no influence on the determination of the above-named magnitudes. The net interest of durable goods, however, is determined, like ground-rent, simply by the value of their useful services (after the cost of repairs has been deducted).

If, however, we disregard the difficulties which we mentioned first, and if in the meantime we suppose that the services of the land and the use of the other rent-goods are *free*—the influence of these factors will be considered later—then Böhm-Bawerk in Volume III, Chapter V, of his book has taught us that with the help of the concept of the length of the production period a very simple relationship between the present position of wages and of capital-interest can be laid down, if the number of the available workers within an economy and the amount of the capital are known. Böhm-Bawerk avoids the use of mathematical symbols here and tries to make the matter clear by presenting it in tabular form. But in doing this he is obliged to assume that the magnitudes in question vary discontinuously. Since, however, the assumption of magnitudes which vary continuously in fact corresponds more nearly to reality as well as being simpler in theory, I for my part prefer to take this assumption as fundamental, and shall present the theory in a corresponding mathematical guise. About Böhm-Bawerk's method of treating these questions, I shall say a few words later.

value; whether it lasts 200 instead of 100 years makes a difference of less than 0·7 per cent; whether it lasts for ever instead of for 200 years, makes absolutely no difference, since only the minute difference in value of 0·0057 per cent is involved (i.e. instead of perhaps 100,000 M the house would then be worth 100,005 M 70 $Pf.$).

4—Capital-interest and wages in the stationary economy

A. Mathematical presentation

Let us therefore assume that a group of workers wish to start a productive undertaking on their own account, in which one commodity or a number of goods is produced *once*. They themselves possess no capital. They can, however, within certain limits, obtain any amount of money on loan at a rate of interest which for the time being we shall think of as *given*. In order to make the matter as simple as possible, we shall assume that they do all the necessary preparatory work themselves, make the tools, and so on. However, once the production process is complete and the goods are ready, these tools are assumed to be worn out and valueless. The more labour they devote to these preparations for production, the lengthier will be the production process. But, as compensation for this, the quantity of goods produced, or rather their value, will be greater, according to our assumptions; and, what is more, this value must here be assumed to be growing in a *greater* proportion than the length of the period of production itself; so that the value of the average (i.e. annual or daily) production of a worker is also to be thought of as growing with the length of the period of production (in which case, however, the scale of the surplus profits is necessarily a decreasing one).

If now we ask what method of production or—what is here the same thing—how long a period of production these workers are to choose with most advantage to themselves, this problem, it is clear, remains vague, since the workers can obviously pursue two different aims: on the one hand, they may strive to attain the greatest possible ultimate profit; on the other, they may desire to procure for themselves a subsistence as abundant as possible *while the work lasts*. But since we still wish to keep the hypothesis of the stationary condition and must consequently regard the sum of the capitals as an invariable magnitude, we can disregard completely the gain which will ultimately result and which would obviously be *a new capital*.[1] We therefore assume that the workers, even when they them-

---

[1] The neglect of this important distinction is, in my opinion (indicated above), one of the fundamental mistakes in Böhm-Bawerk's presentation, which is otherwise so clear. We shall see in due course how he was led by it to criticize in a quite mistaken way Jevons's theory of interest.

selves are the entrepreneurs, merely strive to attain the second of these two aims, the greatest possible subsistence or wages. Then the problem is quite definite and very easy to solve.

Let the value of the final product be s. According to our last assumption, we shall find that this value comprises the whole capital engaged in production plus interest on this capital, and no more. But the capital consists here merely of the cost of maintaining the workers and will consequently amount to $t \cdot l$ for each worker, if l stands for the annual subsistence or annual wage of one worker, still to be determined, and t for the length of the period of production expressed in years (and fractions of years). If now the whole capital was borrowed already at the beginning of the production process, then, on the assumption of simple interest and if z stands for the rate of interest, $t \cdot l \cdot z \cdot t$ (or $t^2 \cdot l \cdot z$) must consequently be paid as interest. But if the capital is only invested by instalments, this sum has to be multiplied by some proper fraction, which in the case of a constant taking-up of capital can, it is evident, become as small as $\frac{1}{2}$, and no smaller. We therefore write

$$s = t \cdot l\left(1 + \frac{zt}{2}\right) \qquad (12)$$

The value $\frac{t}{2}$ can be taken as the average length of the investment of capital, which therefore need only amount to half the length of the process of production, if the production is constant.

If both sides are divided by t, we have, since $\frac{s}{t}$ obviously stands for the *average annual production* of one worker which we shall call p:

$$p = l\left(1 + \frac{z \cdot t}{2}\right) \qquad (13)$$

s and p are here, as has already been said, to be understood as *functions* and, what is more, as *known* functions of t; z is assumed to be a *known* value; and the task is now to determine t in such a way that l becomes *as great as possible*. This is done, of course, by means of differentiating on both sides in respect of t, as if l were a constant; since, in the case of a maximum, $dl = 0.$[1] We consequently obtain

$$\frac{dp}{dt} = \frac{l \cdot z}{2} \tag{14}$$

and this equation gives us, together with (13), the values of t and l, expressed in terms of z, which we require to know.

In order to make the understanding of this problem easier, we shall also illustrate this result geometrically. We assume

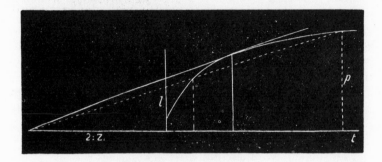

that t and p are abscissa and ordinate of a curve that, according to the known attributes of p, must follow a rising course which, however, is concave in respect of the axis of abscissae and (since something can always be produced, even in production for immediate use which is carried out without any capital) intersects the axis of ordinates at a certain distance from the zero-point. If we take any one point on this curve and connect it by a straight line to a fixed point which lies on the negative side of the axis of abscissae at a distance of $\frac{2}{z}$ from the zero-point, then this straight line will cut off a section of the axis of ordinates which is equal to l, as follows from equation (13) if it is written in the form

$$p : l = \left(\frac{2}{z} + t\right) : \frac{2}{z}$$

The greatest value of l can consequently be attained, if from the

---

[1] That in this case a maximum and not a minimum of l occurs, can, with reference to the conditions of the problem, easily be proved. Compare the following geometrical illustration.

fixed point mentioned a tangent is drawn to the curve. This is just what equation (14) expresses.

Let us now deal with the contrary question. Let us suppose that the wages are given and that an entrepreneur who is himself a capitalist wishes to direct his production in such a way that the greatest possible profit accrues to himself from the capital which he has expended on each of the workers employed and consequently on the whole production. This problem (the only one which Böhm-Bawerk has dealt with) seems at first sight to be quite different from the former, but leads to precisely the same expressions. That is to say, when p and l stand for annual production and annual wages of a worker, we obtain in this case also

$$p = l\left(1 + \frac{zt}{2}\right)$$

Here, however, l is understood as a known value and our task is to determine t in such a way that z becomes a maximum. But the differentiation in respect of t takes place in both cases as if l as well as z were a constant, and we obtain as before

$$\frac{dp}{dt} = \frac{lz}{2}$$

---

[1] If we are to take into consideration compound interest instead of simple interest, it will be best to set out from equation (12). However (on the assumption of immediate interest) this equation then takes the form

$$s = l\int_0^t (1 + z)^t dt$$
$$= l \cdot \frac{(1 + z)^t - 1}{\log \mathrm{nat}\,(1 + z)}$$

which afterwards is combined with its first derivative in respect of t:

$$\frac{ds}{dt} = l(1 + z)^t$$

For sufficiently small values of z and values of t which are not too great, the first expression turns into

$$s = l \cdot \frac{tz + \frac{t(t - 1)}{2}z^2}{z - \frac{z^2}{2}} = lt\left(1 + \frac{z}{2}\right)\left(1 + \frac{t - 1}{2}z\right)$$

$$s = lt\left(1 + \frac{zt}{2}\right)$$

as when calculating simple interest.

Using these equations, t and z can now be expressed in terms of l.

The geometrical solution is arrived at in this case by taking a point at a distance l from the zero-point on the axis of ordinates and drawing from this point a tangent to the curve. This tangent now determines on the negative side of the axis of abscissae the length $\frac{2}{z}$, which in turn determines the value of z. (If, for instance, the length so determined is 40, z becomes equal to $\frac{1}{20}$ or 5 per cent.)

Here it is assumed, however, that the capital is employed only successively. Temporarily, therefore, a use must be found for it *outside* the business. In order to avoid this difficulty, we could imagine that the entrepreneur carries on not merely one, but several businesses of the same kind at the same time, in all of which the period of production is the same, but which are at different stages of progress, so that the entrepreneur can consequently market finished goods once a month, say, or once a week. The proceeds from these provide him with necessary money for the next payment of wages. Since in this case each of the workers employed has, on an average, half of the production process behind him,[1] the average capital invested in each worker obviously amounts to $\frac{t \cdot l}{2}$. But the average monthly production of each worker is $\frac{p}{12}$ and the monthly wage $\frac{l}{12}$, and their difference $\frac{p - l}{12}$ can be regarded as monthly interest on the capital invested in each worker; so that the monthly rate of interest amounts to $\frac{p - l}{6t \cdot l}$, and the yearly rate of interest consequently amounts to $\frac{2(p - l)}{t \cdot l}$, and we obtain

$$z = \frac{2(p - l)}{t \cdot l} \quad \text{or} \quad p = l\left(1 + \frac{tz}{2}\right)$$

as above.

---

[1] Strictly speaking, this is, of course, only correct if the month can be regarded as an infinitely small part of the whole process of production. As regards this whole subject, cf. my essay 'Kapitalzins und Arbeitslohn' in *Conrads Jahrbücher*, December 1893, p. 868 ff.

But it is not necessary to suppose such a rigorously con-
ducted gradation of production within the separate businesses.
It is sufficient if this phenomenon appears as the result of the
total production. This is the same as saying that the different
products and half-finished products are produced precisely
when consumption and production require them. That is to
say, the capital, too, can then find employment through the
mechanism of the loan-market just when it becomes free.[1]

This is more or less the actual state of affairs, or rather it is
the ideal towards which production continually strives. But
this ideal, for several reasons, can only be partly attained.

It was, by the way, assumed in what has just been said, that
production is itself constant, so that at each moment of production the same number of workers is employed. This, too, is
of course not the case. At certain stages of production there
is perhaps room for very few workers or for no workers at all—
when, for instance, the goods in process of production are simply
exposed to the action of natural forces; for example, when
ripening grain continues standing in the fields throughout the
summer, or when, in the production of wine, after the completion of the actual production, the new wine remains lying
in the cellar, perhaps for years. Finally, the period of production
ought actually to be thought of as lasting until the finished
goods are in fact sold.

Still, we shall allow for all these facts if we put the general
expression $\epsilon \cdot t$ (where ϵ is a proper fraction) instead of $\frac{t}{2}$ for
the length of the investment of capital.

It is clear that in this case the gradation of production within
the particular economy must at least be carried to the point
at which the workers employed find uninterrupted occupation.
Our equation (13) can then take the form

$$p = l(1 + \epsilon \cdot t \cdot z)$$

The distribution of labour over the period of production can
itself be altered, however, and ϵ is therefore in reality a variable
quantity. The product $\epsilon \cdot t$, that is to say, the investment period
of the capital, can here, however, be conceived as a single

---

[1] No account is, of course, taken here of brokerage, etc., and a single rate
of interest is assumed for the whole capital market.

variable, so that the expressions undergo no essential alteration, at least when calculating simple interest.

If now, within the branch of the business in question, the total existing capital and the total number of workers employed were each a constant magnitude, we could find out not only the above relations between wage, level of interest and length of the period of production (which, to be sure, can be assumed to be equal practically everywhere within this branch of the business), but even these magnitudes themselves. That is to say, since the capital invested in each worker is, on an average, $\frac{t \cdot l}{2}$ (or more generally $\epsilon \cdot t \cdot l$), we obtain

$$K = \frac{A \cdot l \cdot t}{2} \qquad (15)$$

when K stands for the total capital and A for the number of workers employed. Using this equation in combination with the equations (13) and (14), we can express l, t and z in terms of K and A. We obtain, in fact, from (13) and (14), by eliminating z,

$$p = l + t\frac{dp}{dt} \qquad (16)$$

and if the value of l obtained from the above equation is substituted in (15), we get

$$K = \frac{A}{2}\left(tp - t^2\frac{dp}{dt}\right) \qquad (17)$$

This equation can be solved for t, since p and $\frac{dp}{dt}$ must be thought of as known functions of t; and so forth.

This assumption, however, will not do. Capital and labour which are to-day employed in the manufacture of goods of a certain kind, can to-morrow have been partly transferred to other branches of business. Within the whole economy, however, the number of available workers and the total capital can be regarded as approximately given magnitudes. If, therefore, following Böhm-Bawerk's precedent, we may assume as a first approximation within all branches of the business *the same* productivity and the same *increase* in productivity when the length of the period of production is increased, then, obviously, our equations set forth above can be regarded as valid for the whole economy, since t stands for the length of the period of production, p the yearly production of one worker, and l and z the wage and the level of interest. According to our assumption, these values must be the same in all the businesses.

Indeed, in practical life the fulfilment of these equations would take place in the following way. At each level of wages a period of production of a certain length proves to be the most advantageous to the entrepreneur-capitalists, since it promises the greatest possible interest (makes z a maximum). If in this case all the workers find employment and the whole of the existing capital is invested, these proportions will undergo no further change: equilibrium on the capital-labour market has been reached. But if more labour is demanded than is available, wages must rise. At the new level of wages a new and, what is more, a *longer* period of production proves at once to be the most profitable, as is evident, and the superfluous capital is absorbed partly by the rise in wages, and partly by the lengthening of the period of production.

If, on the other hand, more labour is available than can be employed during a period of production of the length in question, wages must fall, owing to competition of the workers. At this lower level of wages a new and, what is more, a *shorter* period of production recommends itself as the one which is now most profitable to the capitalists. This is adopted, and the capital which was before insufficient is now able to give employment to all workers, partly owing to the decrease in wages, but partly also to the shortened period of production.

In both cases equilibrium is finally achieved, although only after several oscillations in this and that direction; and in the case of equilibrium all our above equations are fulfilled.

If, on the contrary, we had set out from the assumption that the workers are themselves entrepreneurs, the result would have been the same—with this difference, however, that supply and demand now occur on the loan market, so that the rising or falling rate of interest now takes the place of increasing and decreasing wages.

In both cases the equations of equilibrium will be the same, and, what is more, a large amount of capital and a comparatively small number of workers will always be connected with a longer period of production, high wages and a low rate of interest—and vice versa. That is to say, when the capitalists are entrepreneurs, the lengthening of the period of production is seen to be a *reaction* on the part of the capitalists against the increase in wages which has taken place and the low rate of interest *which results therefrom*. But as a result of this lengthening of the period, interest can again be raised to some extent, but cannot reach the level achieved in the case of the previous lower level of wages.

If, on the contrary, the workers are entrepreneurs, and the rate of interest, due to increased demand for capital, has risen, the workers will shorten the period of production, and by this means once again be able to improve to some extent their incomes (i.e. wages), diminished by the rise in interest. But neither wages nor interest can in this case return to quite the former position.[1]

The question could be asked, how far the above result is affected by the existence of people who work with their own capital. This question is, however, easily answered. If such a worker has enough capital to observe (in the case of steadily-flowing production)[2] the usual period of production, then he will select just this period (always supposing that his purpose is merely to conserve his capital and not to increase it). If he has less capital, he must adopt a shorter period of production; if he has more, then he *can*, if he so desires, adopt a longer period. In both cases, however, he will obtain a greater income if he chooses the customary period of production. In order to do so, he will, in the first case, procure the capital which he still requires by means of a loan at the ordinary rate of interest, and in the second case he will lend the superfluous capital or use it to employ other workers. For the validity of our formulae it is therefore of no consequence whatever *who* possesses the capital, provided only that the latter is employed as capital.

Here, however, I must draw attention to a certain ambiguity in the problem, which was not taken into consideration by Böhm-Bawerk and which I in my criticism of his presentation (in *Conrads Jahrbücher*, December 1892) had not yet noticed.

One could imagine capitalists adopting longer and longer periods of production in a quite haphazard way, wages being

[1] We can easily convince ourselves of the truth of this, either by examining equations (13) and (14), or, still more easily, by considering the relevant diagram.

[2] This gradation of production can, of course, be very easily adopted by individual producers as well. Agriculture and, still more, market-gardening are examples.

in this case determined every time by the competition of capitalists and workers according to equation (15),

$$K = \frac{A \cdot l \cdot t}{2}$$

The interest attained is still given by (13),

$$p = l\left(1 + \frac{t \cdot z}{2}\right)$$

but since l is now no longer regarded as a constant but depends, according to (15), on t, it follows that when we try to determine t in such a way that z becomes a maximum, we are led (as can easily be seen) not to equation (14) but to the quite different equation

$$\frac{dp}{dt} = -\frac{l}{t}$$

Since l and t are essentially positive, $\frac{dp}{dt}$ would have to be negative here; that is to say, supposing the length of production is increased more and more, the greatest possible interest will only be attained when the scale of productivity (the annual production of one worker) has changed into a decreasing one. Practically speaking, no real maximum of the rate of interest consequently exists here, but *each* lengthening of the period of production will be advantageous to the capitalists.

This result may seem strange, but is not difficult to understand. What we have been considering above was the case of *free* competition, where everyone pursues his own advantage. But our last assumption presupposes that capitalists combine to depress wages and that the workers can do nothing about this. But then each lengthening of production will prove in the end to be remunerative, provided it is undertaken simultaneously in all businesses; since the wage-capital available for each year is diminished and wages must consequently fall. Even if the productivity of one worker remains unaltered or even undergoes a slight decline, it will still be remunerative. In this case, of course, the fall in wages will sooner or later cause, somehow or other, a drop in the number of workers within the economy, or the workers must be partly supported by charity. But if this point has not yet been reached, it will always be in the interest of the capitalists *as a class* to extend the period of production.

But the situation is different if there is free competition between the capitalists, because in this case the low level of wages will be a temptation to every individual capitalist to shorten the period of production and to use his capital for the employment of a greater number of workers. But if several capitalists do this, wages will, of course, rise.

On the other hand, by sticking together, workers can, within certain limits, undoubtedly enforce a shorter period of production if, for instance, they refuse to work with the new 'labour-saving' machines. As a result of this, wages will rise— if, of course, we assume that the capital remains undiminished in spite of the lower rate of interest. But if there is free competition amongst workers, this reduced rate of interest will, for some workers, be a temptation to become entrepreneurs themselves—and, what is more, according to the lower level of interest—by adopting longer periods of production. And so the demand for capital would again become greater, etc. We cannot pursue this subject further here. However, what has been said will suffice to show that the new concept 'period of production' seems destined to bring order and clarity to some of the most complicated problems of political economy, problems which are far from being explained.

B. Böhm-Bawerk's presentation and his 'positive' law of interest. His criticism of Jevons's theory of interest

The above-mentioned presentation is substantially identical with the theory to which Böhm-Bawerk has devoted the last chapter of his book. But this theory obviously contains merely an *element* of a complete theory of interest, because, on the one hand, the services of the land (actually the services of all rent-goods) were left unconsidered, and because, on the other hand, the theory assumes that there is an identical productivity and scale of productiveness for all branches of production —which is very far from reality. In what follows I shall try to replace this theory by another, which is complete in both these respects; and in this way I hope, in the end, to be able to take up again our problem of determining the exchange value, which was not brought to a conclusion in the previous chapter.

First of all, however, I shall go a little more deeply into Böhm-Bawerk's treatment of this problem, in order to emphasize once again the great importance of this theory, but also because of several remarks which he makes, as it seems to me that his reasoning there does not hold good in all points.

Böhm-Bawerk lays down as an hypothesis an invariable pattern, which is supposed to represent the productiveness of production when, for instance, a period of production of one, two, three, etc., years is adopted. After this he shows how, assuming different levels of wages, now this and now that period of production yields the highest interest on the capital which has to be invested in each worker. I reproduce here one of the relevant tables. This corresponds to just *the* level of wages, 500 fl., which would prove absolutely right for the number of workers and amount of capital chosen in this example.

Level of wage 500 fl.

Period of production	Product of one working-year	Annual profit per worker	Number of employed	Total annual profit on each 10,000 fl.
1 year	350 fl.	− 150 fl.	40	(Loss)
2 years	450 ,,	− 50 ,,	20	,,
3 ,,	530 ,,	30 ,,	13·33	400·00 fl.
4 ,,	580 ,,	80 ,,	10	800·00 ,,
5 ,,	620 ,,	120 ,,	8	960·00 ,,
6 ,,	650 ,,	150 ,,	6·66	**1,000·00** ,,
7 ,,	670 ,,	170 ,,	5·71	970·70 fl.
8 ,,	685 ,,	185 ,,	5	925·00 ,,
9 ,,	695 ,,	195 ,,	4·44	866·66 fl.
10 ,,	700 ,,	200 ,,	4	800·00 ,,

The first three columns require no explanation. The fourth column shows the number of workers that can be employed with a capital of 10,000 fl. in a period of production of 1, 2, 3, etc., years respectively; in which case it is assumed that the advance of capital amounts to only *half* the sum of wages paid during the period of production—as will really be the case if there is an appropriate 'gradation' of production and payment of wages. If, therefore, the period of production is x years, the figures in this column are determined by the formula

$$10,000 : \frac{x \cdot 500}{2} = \frac{40}{x}$$

The fifth column can now be obtained by multiplying the appropriate figures of the third and fourth columns. Its figures give, therefore, for each year, the profit on 10,000 fl., or, divided by 100, the level of interest, expressed in percentages.[1]

From this table we see that, when the rate of wage is 500 fl., the adoption of a period of production of *six years* will yield the highest interest on the invested capital, i.e. 10 per cent, whilst a period of five years would yield only 9·6 per cent, and a period of seven years only 9·7 per cent. This depends entirely, however, upon the level of wages. In the same way we see that, at a rate of wage of only 300 fl., and under otherwise identical circumstances, a period of production of only *three* years would prove the most profitable, and the capital would even yield interest at the rate of 51 per cent. At a rate of wage of 600 fl., on the other hand, a production period of *eight* years must be selected, 'which will yield the modest, but still advantageous interest of 3·54 per cent.'[2]

If now—as the author for the sake of argument supposes— a national capital of 15,000 million *gulden* and 10 million workers are available, then, at a rate of wage of 500 fl. and with the correspondingly most advantageous production period of six years, the market will be in equilibrium. In other words, the existing capital will be just sufficient to keep all these workers fully occupied (and vice versa), since

$$10 \text{ million} \times \frac{6}{2} \times 500 \text{ fl.} = 15,000 \text{ million fl.}$$

And this state of equilibrium will necessarily also arise of its own accord through the competition of workers and capitalists. If, that is to say, wages were somewhat higher, i.e. 510 fl., then the six-year production period would still be the most remunerative. However, with the existing capital of 15,000 million fl., only 9,800,000 workers could be employed, 'and the unemployed

---

[1] The figures of the third column, divided by the number of years of the period of production in question, represent the interest, calculated for half the level of wages; for the necessary advance of capital for each worker over a period of x years is $\frac{x}{2}$ of the yearly wage, and the annual profit from one worker constitutes the interest on this sum. For example, if the period is one of six years, we obtain

$$\frac{150}{6} : 250 = 10 : 100$$

[2] Loc. cit., p. 415.

remainder, by creating a situation in which supply far exceeds demand, would exert pressure on the price of labour, until such time as they themselves can be, and are, employed'; which can only happen at a rate of wage of 500 fl. (This superfluity of workers shows itself, of course, in a much more marked degree when the rise in the rate of wages leads also to a lengthening of the period of production, which in our example will only be the case when the rate of wages is 530 fl. or more. It will, however, *always* be the case if we assume a continuously variable period of production.) If, on the contrary, the wage were a little lower, say 490 fl., then only 14,700 million fl. capital would be taken up by the employment of the existing 10 million workers. The unemployed remainder would then obtain employment through overbidding, and the result would again be a rise in wages which would continue until the point was finally reached at which everything can and does come into equilibrium.

So far everything seems to be correct.[1] The agreement with our formulae set forth above will be clear to every mathematically-trained reader. Strange to say, however, Böhm-Bawerk believes that he has found in the series of numbers which he has set down 'other relationships as well, which in a *positive* (?) way point to the resulting rate of interest of 10 per cent and which can provide the material for a positive law of the level of interest.' I reproduce here literally what he has to say on this subject.

"To arrive at the position of equilibrium, the capital of the community had to be withdrawn from the shorter processes of production, in which full employment could not have been found for it with the existing stock of labour, and employed in gradually lengthening processes, until it was fully occupied. This happened in a six-year period of production. On the other hand, the adoption of still longer processes, for which the capital would *not* have been sufficient, had, economically, to be

---

[1] Here, however, we must remember the situation mentioned on p. 128 ff. Certainly, *when competition is free*, a rate of wage of 500 fl. comes about in the way described above, and at this rate the six-year period of production is seen to be the most profitable for each individual capitalist. If, however, the capitalists, regardless of this, agree to adopt a seven-year period, then the wage would have to fall to about 430 fl., and at *this* rate of wage the seven-year period will now yield a net profit of more than 16 per cent. The profit would be still more huge if an eight-year period were adopted, and so forth.

prevented. In these circumstances the producers who adopt the six-year period of production are the last buyers, the 'marginal buyers'; the producers who would like to adopt a seven-year period of production are the most capable excluded suitors for means of subsistence; and, according to the well-known law, the price that results must fall between the subjective valuations of these two. How does it stand with the valuations?

"What we have to consider is simply this: *What is the utility which, for these two sets of buyers, depends on the disposal over a definite sum of means of subsistence?* First of all, the general assertion must be made, that on the disposal over each half-year's wage—in the present case 250 fl.—depends *one year's* extension of the production period per worker.[1] Thus the ability to embark on or continue in the six-year, instead of the shorter five-year period of production, employing one labourer, depends, especially for the producers who adopt the six-year period, on the possession or non-possession of 250 fl.; and since, according to our scheme of productivity, the year's product from one worker in a five-year production period amounts to only 620 fl., whereas in a six-year period it amounts to 650 fl., the attainment of an annual surplus product of **30 fl.** depends, for the marginal buyers, on their having at their disposal 250 fl. On the other hand, those would-be producers who try to take means of subsistence out of the market, in order to extend the production period to seven years even, could gain by this extension only a surplus return of **20 fl.** (670 − 650 fl.) . . .

"If, therefore—and this is indispensable to the attainment of equilibrium—the extension of the production period is to halt at the limit of six years, the agio established by the fixing of the price (i.e. the interest) must lie between the rate that corresponds to the valuation of the last buyers (30 fl. on 250 fl., or 12 per

---

[1] Böhm-Bawerk gives in a note (p. 419) 'the mathematical proof of this somewhat paradoxical thesis,' assuming a '*five*-year production divided into sections of one year each.' If, however, we assume—as in other contexts he himself does—a continuous gradation of production and wage-payment, then what was assumed above becomes self-evident; for a production of n years will then require for every worker, as was pointed out above, an advance of capital of $\frac{n}{2}$ yearly wages. A production of $n + 1$ years consequently requires an advance of $\frac{n + 1}{2}$ yearly wages, and the difference between these figures is precisely half the yearly wage.

cent) as *upper limit*, and the rate of 8 per cent, corresponding to the valuation of the competitors first excluded, as *lower limit*. . . . The fact that, within these bounds, a rate of interest of 10 per cent was precisely indicated, is, of course, no longer due to the limiting effect of the valuations of the marginal pairs, but, as described on p. 226 ff., simply to the quantitative effect of supply and demand."

All this sounds very clear and convincing, to be sure. But, when we look at it more closely, it unfortunately no longer seems clear. How could a surplus return of 30 fl., i.e. a net profit of 12 per cent, depend, for the producers who have adopted the six-year period, on their having the disposal over 250 fl.? we are obliged to ask; since at the assumed rate of wage of 500 fl. the capital can, *at most*, yield an interest of 10 per cent! And vice versa: if they can obtain this net profit, why should 'supply and demand' depress the interest which has to be paid to only 10 per cent? This could only occur if the capital sufficed for *more* than a six-year period, which, however, was not the case. But as a matter of fact a net profit of only 25 fl., or just 10 per cent, depends, for the producers who wish to go over, at the rate of wage mentioned, from the five-year to the six-year period, on having at their disposal 250 fl.; the remaining 5 fl. of the surplus return are due to the fact that their capital, which was already employed before, and which in the five-year period amounted to 5×250 fl. per worker, is now employed in a six-year period of production where it now yields 10 per cent instead of only 9·6 per cent. For 5×250 fl. it consequently yields 125 fl. instead of 120 fl.

And *this* increase of profits they could obtain in any case, even *without* having new capital at their disposal, if they only decreased the number of their workers in a corresponding proportion.

Likewise, an added capital of 250 fl. would yield, when changing over to a seven-year period, not only 20 fl., but more than 24 fl. But at the same time the capital which was previously employed in the six-year period will have to be content with an interest of only 9·7 per cent instead of 10 per cent.

It is, therefore, certainly true that interest, calculated for half the level of wage, comes to lie 'between the surplus return of the last permissible extension of production and that of the no longer permissible extension of production'; but between these limits its definite level is not determined by supply and demand but simply by the productiveness of the most profitable period of production. Whether in this case *wages* will really remain at the assumed rate or can be kept there, will depend on the supply and demand situation with regard to labour. This, however, is quite a different question.[1]

The idea of regarding the 'producers who adopt the six-year period of production' as 'the last buyers,' etc., must be regarded as altogether wrong, for, at the rate of wage in question, *everybody* will choose this period, and neither a longer nor a shorter one. It would, indeed, not be impossible to conceive the present problem also as one which involves an exchange between present and future goods—with this reservation, however, that the exchange is an alternative one, in that the length of the period of production to be chosen influences the quantity of the future commodity (the average annual production) as well as that of the present commodity (namely the wage-capital to be employed in the present year). But we shall not dwell longer upon this.

When the length of the process of production can be changed by indefinitely small steps, as is for the most part really the case in practical life, the productiveness of the last small step that can actually be taken, and the productiveness of the step which is just out of reach, approach each other closely. Böhm-Bawerk therefore believes that he is able 'to formulate the law of the level of interest in such a way that this level is determined *by the surplus return of the last still permitted extension of production*'; and in his controversy with Jevons (p. 427, note) he remarks that 'the level of the rate of interest is to be deduced from the relation of the last surplus return to the sum of subsistence which allows the last extension of production.'

Without further qualification, however, the last statement is misleading. The words 'at an unchanged rate of wage' need to be added to it, and the word 'allows' should be replaced by 'brings about' or some such phrase. But then this statement simply expresses a consequence of the fact that the highest possible level of interest is already reached, and throws no further light on the nature of interest. One could, however, be

[1] The passage on p. 226 ff. quoted by Böhm-Bawerk refers to the capital-labour market, where capitalists and workers offer to each other, within certain limits, their 'goods' '*at any price*,' and where, therefore, the proportion of exchange (the wage) simply becomes equal to the proportion of the existing quantities.

led by the wording of the sentence to believe that, if an increase in the national capital leads to an extension of the period of production, the number of workers remaining the same, then the surplus return obtained through *this* extension, divided by the capital increase in question, will give us approximately the level of interest. This would be decidedly wrong. The result of this division sum is, as we shall see, always *smaller* than the interest and, what is more, it is smaller by a *finite* amount, even when it is a question of a minimum change. This is connected with the fact that this increase in the national capital is accompanied by an increase in wages which partially swallows it up, with the result that the lengthening of production actually achieved always falls short of the lengthening of production possible when the rate of wage remains unchanged.

With the help of the equations which we used before, this can be shown quite easily, and further relationships between the values occurring here, which might not be without interest, can be stated.

If p is replaced by $F(t)$ and $\dfrac{dp}{dt}$ by $F'(t)$, then, generally speaking

$$F(t) - F(t - \Delta t) > F'(t)\Delta t > F(t + \Delta t) - F(t)$$

since $F(t)$ is an increasing, and $F'(t)$, on the contrary, a decreasing function of t. Here Δt stands for a small quantity of time. Now, according to (14), when the level of interest reaches a maximum,

$$F'(t) = \frac{lz}{2}$$

We therefore obtain for the corresponding value of t

$$F(t) - F(t - \Delta t) > \frac{l \cdot \Delta t}{2} \cdot z > F(t + \Delta t) - F(t)$$

In this inequality Böhm-Bawerk's rules stated above find expression, since an extension of the period of production amounting to Δt requires a new capital investment per worker of $\dfrac{l \cdot \Delta t}{2}$.[1]

---

[1] That is to say, the capital formerly employed was $\dfrac{lt}{2}$ per worker; the capital now employed is consequently $\dfrac{l(t + \Delta t)}{2}$, and the difference between these expressions amounts to $\dfrac{l \cdot \Delta t}{2}$.

In the case of a given national capital and a given number of workers, the length of the period of production and the wage are found, as we have seen, by means of the equations

$$K = \frac{A \cdot l \cdot t}{2} \tag{15}$$

and

$$l = p - tp' \tag{16}$$

in which p' replaces $dp : dt$. The rate of interest proper to them is then given by one or other of the identical expressions

$$z = (p - l) : \frac{tl}{2} = p' : \frac{l}{2}$$

If, however, the total capital is slightly increased, whilst the number of workers remains the same, a *new* state of equilibrium is reached, with a change in the level of wage and in the length of the period of production; with the result that, when K becomes $K + dK$, l is changed to $l + dl$ and t to $t + dt$. The relationships between the quantities dK, dl and dt are found simply by differentiation of the above equations (15) and (16), namely

$$dK = \frac{A}{2}(l dt + t dl) \tag{18}$$

and

$$dl = - tp'' dt \tag{19}$$

where p'' is written for $\dfrac{d^2p}{dt^2}$. We shall now apply these equations in various ways.

The annual production p of one worker undergoes, when t becomes $t + dt$, the increase dp or $p' dt$; the total surplus return is consequently $A \cdot p' dt$. If we want to find out the proportion of this quantity to the increase in the national capital, we obtain from (18) and (19)

$$\frac{A \cdot p' dt}{dK} = \frac{2p' dt}{l dt + t dl} = \frac{2p'}{l - t^2 p''}$$

Since p'' is always *negative*, the latter expression will always be smaller than $\dfrac{2p'}{l}$ —that is to say, smaller than the rate of interest, as I have remarked above.

In the case of a relative increase of the national capital the wage increases and the level of interest decreases. This circumstance is generally explained by the fact that, with increasingly capitalistic production, the workers' *share* in the result of the production becomes greater and greater, whilst that of the capital becomes smaller and smaller. This, however, is not unconditionally true. It might very well happen that the workers, although they now have higher wages, nevertheless obtain a *smaller* share in the production, since its productiveness has in the meantime increased; or—which is the same thing— the share of the capitalists might be greater, although this share amounts to a smaller interest on the capital, which in the meantime has increased. In order to be able to decide whether this is really the case or not, we must see whether the expression $\dfrac{l}{p}$ increases or decreases when t increases, that is to say, whether

$$p\frac{dl}{dt} - lp'$$

is positive or negative.

Taking into account the equations (19) and (16), this expression becomes

$$- tp'' \cdot p + t(p')^2 - p' \cdot p$$

The first two terms of the expression are positive (since $p'' < 0$); the third term, on the contrary, is negative. In certain circumstances, therefore, the sum of the three terms can be positive or negative.

For example, at a rate of wage of 280 fl. a two-year period of production would be the most remunerative (if we base our calculations upon Böhm-Bawerk's figures). At a rate of wage of 300 fl., on the other hand, a three-year period would be the most remunerative. The annual production of one worker in the two-year period was 450 fl., in the three-year period, on the other hand, 530 fl. Now 280 : 450 > 300 : 530. If, consequently, the period of production is here extended from two to three years through a corresponding increase in capital, the share of the capitalists in the production *increases* and the share of the workers decreases, in spite of the fact that the wages have risen and the capital-interest has decreased. If, on the contrary, it is a question of periods of production of greater length, every new extension of the period of production will, in general, diminish the share of the capitalists and increase that of the workers.

But, finally, the question could be raised, to what extent the net profit of the capitalists—will, in fact, increase when the capital is increased and the period of production is extended. This is obviously a question of the greatest practical significance. If, that is to say, an increase in capital merely helped to diminish the profit on the capital, then such a capital increase would conflict with the interests of the capitalists as a class and would probably be prevented in some way or other. On the other hand, every increase in capital is, of course, advantageous to the workers. The result would be that the interests of the capitalists and the workers, which in this respect hitherto went hand in hand to some extent, would now clash.

The yearly profit on each worker was $p - l$. When t becomes $t + dt$, this quantity undergoes the change

$$d(p - l) = p'dt - dl$$

or, taking into account (19),

$$= (p' + tp'')dt$$

The solution of our problem consequently depends on whether the latter expression is positive or negative. p' is positive; p'', on the contrary, is negative. If now p'' (taken positively) is very small, that is to say, if p' is approximately constant, so that each extension of the period of production yields nearly the same surplus return, then the expression becomes positive. Every extension of the period of production and every increase of the national capital will then increase the net profit also (although, of course, not in the same proportion as the capital itself increases). If, on the other hand, p'' is relatively big, that is to say, if p' decreases rapidly, then the expression becomes finally negative: the surplus return of the extended period of production is *more* than counterbalanced by the increase of wages.

If we suppose that p increases with t in a logarithmic proportion, so that $p = \alpha + \beta \log$ nat t, where α and β are constants, then $p' = \dfrac{\beta}{t}$ and $p'' = -\dfrac{\beta}{t^2}$; we therefore now have for *every* value of t

$$p' + tp'' = 0$$

The net profit, then, remains constant, even if the period of production is lengthened to a very great extent by continuous formation of capital: a national capital of 15,000 million fl. does not yield more than a capital of 1,500 or even of 150 million fl.— provided the number of workers is always assumed to be unchanged. But if p increases in a greater proportion, then, in the case of an extended period of production, the net profit increases also. If, on the other hand, p increases in a smaller proportion,[1] then the absolute net profit decreases with every new increase of capital and lengthening of production. If we base our calculations on the figures of productiveness given in the table, we see, for instance, that if the capital increases from 15 milliards fl. to $19\frac{1}{4}$ milliards fl., then, at the new rate of wage of 550 fl., the seven-year period would prove to be the most profitable one. But the annual profit from each worker would then amount to only $(670 - 550) = 120$ fl. instead of the 150 fl. obtained before, and the total net profit would, of course, diminish in the same proportion.

The figures in the table are, to be sure, only examples, but the decreasing scale of surplus returns which characterizes them may be regarded as a well-established fact or, rather, a matter of course. Sooner or later, if the formation of capital is continued and if the population remains relatively unchanged, the point *must* therefore be reached, at which the increasing capital is not only accompanied by a fall in the rate of interest, and not only has to be content with a smaller quota of the total production, but even leads to a smaller amount of the total profit; so that every new accumulation of capital directly damages the capitalists—always assuming, of course, completely free competition of capitalists.

As is well known, Thünen had already laid down a law of the level of interest, analogous to his familiar proposition which stated that the average wage[2] depended on the 'yield of the last worker.' According to this law, the level of the rate of

[1] This *must* in the end be the case, since, if t increases, even the expression $\alpha + \beta \log$ nat t increases beyond all limits.

[2] This must not be confused with his well-known but mistaken speculations about the so-called *natural* wage.

interest depends on the productiveness of the 'last invested particle of capital.' The agreement of this theorem with Böhm-Bawerk's own is obvious and is rightly emphasized by the latter. Only it must be remembered that here it is always a question of the capital investments of the individual entrepreneurs only, in which case the wage can and must be assumed to be given.[1] This theorem can by no means be applied to the increase in the national capital itself and to the surplus return brought about thereby.

Jevons in his *Theory of Political Economy* (2nd edition, p. 266) sets out from somewhat different considerations, in order to arrive at a general formula for the level of the rate of interest. Jevons supposes that, when the actual production is completed, the value of the product goes on rising for a while (for example, through its being exposed to the influence of the free forces of nature, as wine lying in the cellar; or because the sale conditions have improved in the meantime). So then the increase in value, taking place at each moment of time, can be thought of as the natural interest on the value which the product possessed at the beginning of this moment of time. If, therefore, $F(t)$ denotes the value of the product after a certain length of time t has elapsed, and $F'(t)$ stands for its derivative, the level of this interest is expressed by the following equation:

$$\text{natural interest} = \frac{F'(t)}{F(t)}$$

Under the assumptions which Jevons makes, this formula is not incorrect, but it is still rather meaningless, for it says nothing about the way in which this natural, continuously variable rate of interest becomes the decisive factor for the interest actually gained. In Jevons's works the problem of the increase of the rate of interest to a maximum, and the relationships between interest and wages, are nowhere discussed.

However, the above-mentioned formula could also quite well be chosen as a point of departure, and is even the most natural starting point if we wish to take compound interest into consideration. But in this case, if it is a question of a continuous

---

[1] Or vice versa: If the workers themselves are entrepreneurs, it must be assumed that the rate of interest is given and that the wage is still to be determined.

production, the labour element and wage element which have been added in each case must be taken into consideration too.[1]

Böhm-Bawerk, as can be seen from his criticism of Jevons's theory (*Positive Theorie*, p. 427, footnote), has completely misunderstood the latter's train of thought, and reproaches him without reason for an 'error' or an 'oversight in principle.'

The 'concrete example' which Böhm-Bawerk uses to illustrate the 'bearing of this oversight' is badly devised and shows that Böhm-Bawerk, as was pointed out before, has himself not arrived at a perfectly clear understanding of the necessary conditions of the problem. He says: 'Let us suppose the case of an entrepreneur whose means would allow him to carry through an eight-year production period with a yearly return of 685 fl., who, by a loan of 300 fl., which would guarantee him subsistence for a ninth (?), is put in a position to go over to a nine-year production period with a return of 695, or a surplus

[1] If a certain capital k is invested, and then t years elapse before the product—which all this time has grown in value—is sold, we obtain

$$s = k(1 + z)^t$$

where s is the final value of the product and z the average yearly rate of interest. This rate of interest becomes a maximum when

$$\frac{ds}{dt} = k(1 + z)^t \cdot \log \text{nat}\,(1 + z).$$

By division of these equations we obtain

$$\frac{ds}{dt} : s = \log \text{nat}\,(1 + z)$$
$$= z - \frac{z^2}{2} + \frac{z^3}{3} - \cdots$$

Since, now, $\log \text{nat}\,(1 + z)$ expresses the 'instantaneous' rate of interest, where z is the yearly rate of interest, Jevons's rule could be completed in such a way that, when interest becomes a maximum, the 'natural' rate of interest must ultimately correspond to the present rate of interest. (For small values of z, $\log \text{nat}\,(1 + z)$ is approximately equal to z.)

If, on the other hand, we assume that production is continuous, we obtain from the two equations in the footnote on p. 123, as can easily be seen,

$$\log \text{nat}\,(1 + z) = \left(\frac{ds}{dt} - l\right) : s$$
or
$$= \frac{ds - l\,dt}{dt} : s.$$

Here, too, it is most advantageous to extend the period of production up to the point at which the (paid out or received) interest (instantaneous rate of interest) is equal to 'the rate of increase of produce divided by the whole produce,' according to Jevons's formula except that in this case the amount of wages which has to be paid each moment must be subtracted from the gross increase of produce.

return of 10 fl. According to Jevons, the rate of interest here should be 10 : 685, or 1·46 per cent. But clearly there is no reason whatever why the suitor for the loan should be ready to offer 10 fl. per year and no more as interest for a sum of 685 fl. It is not the sum of 685 fl., but that of 300 fl., acquisition of which makes the extension of production possible,' etc. According to Böhm-Bawerk, 'an interest of 10 fl. on 300 fl., i.e. $3\frac{1}{3}$ per cent—or even, assuming a steadily-flowing production, a rate of 10 fl. on 150 fl., i.e. $6\frac{2}{3}$ per cent—would be economically possible.'

It is obvious that Jevons has been misunderstood here. But, what is more, where does Böhm-Bawerk get his figure of 300 fl. from? How does he know that the entrepreneur, who before used to earn 685 fl. a year, will be content for a whole year with the very small subsistence of 300 fl.?

In fact, the problem is *unsolved* so long as it is not known how much of his income the entrepreneur in question is accustomed to save. The *simplest* hypothesis is, however, that he does not save anything, but merely preserves his existing capital, that is to say, creates it afresh from period to period. But then his yearly subsistence and the average yearly return from his production (when he only works with his own means) are simply *identical magnitudes*; for his investment of capital would then merely consist in the fact that he supplies himself with his own subsistence while the work lasts; and in the final product he gets back the value of this amount of means of subsistence, neither more nor less. In the case of steadily-flowing production only half the sum of subsistence is necessary as capital. Consequently, for a one-year extension of production, an increase of capital of 685 : 2 = 342½ fl. is necessary. But for this sum he will be able to pay *at most* 10 fl. per year as interest; so that *at the very best* a rate of interest of 2·92 per cent is 'economically possible' under the assumptions here made.

Instead of this simplest hypothesis, we could, of course, make any other assumption about the dispositions of this entrepreneur in general. But if no definite assumption of this kind is made at all, the whole problem obviously lacks a solid basis.

C. Böhm-Bawerk's theory and the wage fund theory

After my efforts to give to Böhm-Bawerk's presentation greater precision and to clarify what is obscure in it, I should like to draw attention once again to the great importance of his theory. As the author himself has explained, this importance consists partly in the fact that in this theory for the first time a real substitute is provided for the obsolete wage fund theory, which several writers have tried to overthrow by cheap criticism without being able to replace it by a better.

The wage fund theory, as is well known, represented the wage as equal to the results of dividing the capital destined for the payment of wages by the number of workers. Now it was pointed out with good reason by the opponents of this theory, that the first of these magnitudes is from the very start completely undetermined. For from the very first it is uncertain how much of the existing national capital will be used productively; nor will the whole of the capital used productively be paid out as wages. Rather, it is more or less 'permanently' invested in buildings, machines, tools, raw materials and half-finished products of all kinds.

The first objection applies equally well to Böhm-Bawerk's theory and can only be removed by a comprehensive theory of savings and capital formation. As for the latter objection, it was clear from the beginning that the actual division of productive capital into means of labour and means of subsistence (into, shall we say, fixed and variable capital) is not arbitrary, but takes place according to the principle of the greatest possible profit; but no one has been able to say anything more definite on this subject. This gap has now been brilliantly bridged by Böhm-Bawerk's theory, which introduces the length of the period of production as one of the factors of the problem and replaces the vague 'wage capital' by the whole national capital, which is relatively definite.

Let us now return to mathematical language. While, according to the wage fund theory, the relationship between wage, number of workers and 'capital' is expressed by the equation

$$l = \frac{K}{A}$$

which leaves nothing to be desired in the matter of simplicity but has this drawback, that it gives only a single relation for two quantities which have to be determined, the new theory expresses these relationships by the equation

$$K = \frac{A \cdot l \cdot t}{2}$$

in which, however, K is now the relatively known magnitude of the total national capital productively used. Here, too, in order to determine the new unknown t, the further relation

$$z = (p - l) : \frac{lt}{2} = \text{maximum}$$

or, which is the same thing,

$$l = p + t \cdot \frac{dp}{dt}$$

is added.

The boundary between fixed and variable capital is in this case really abolished.[1] The whole capital, at least in so far as it is 'turned over' during the period of production, will subsequently appear in the form of money and means of subsistence, and, when no account is taken of ground-rent and the like, will be paid out in wages up to the last penny, but, as Böhm-Bawerk rightly remarks, not *in one year*, but during a period of time which, incidentally, amounts to half the length of the period of production.

5—Completion of Böhm-Bawerk's theory. Capital-interest, wage and rent in their relationship to each other

Böhm-Bawerk's theory forms, as was remarked above, only one element in the complete determination of the level of interest. The main reason for this is that the operation of natural forces, i.e. the services of the land, are not taken into consideration or, rather, are regarded as *free*. However, it would not be impossible to consider this factor also,[2] particularly as the services of the land with regard to capital behave, in several respects, exactly like labour. The landowners, too, get their rent in advance,

---

[1] But only, as I understand it, if we exclude predominantly durable goods (such as buildings, streets, railways, etc.), with which we shall deal soon.

[2] For the time being we shall leave out of account the services of the remaining 'rent-goods.'

before the products are ready for the market. We can even assume, for the sake of simplicity, that ground-rent is paid by instalments, just as wages are; so that here also the necessary advance of capital comprises, on an average, half the length of the period of production.

In what has been said above we have assumed with Böhm-Bawerk, as the simplest hypothesis, that all labour is paid at the same rate and that in all branches of production the scale of surplus returns is the same, so that one and the same period of production is adopted everywhere. In the same way we can assume as a first approximation, that landed property everywhere is of the same quality and that in all branches of production an equally large area of land is required for each worker. The problem is then susceptible of exact treatment in its broadened form also, and we can generalize our equations, laid down above, in such a way that they also include the factor which has now been added.

Let us express the yearly wage by l, as before, and the ground-rent per hectare by r. If now h hectares of land are required for each worker, it is obvious that the capital advanced, calculated for a single worker, amounts in a t-year production to $\frac{t}{2} \cdot (l + h \cdot r)$. This is analogous to what has been said before.

Here the yearly production of one worker depends not only on the length of the period of production, but also, obviously, on the size of the area of land which falls to him. In other words, this magnitude becomes here a function of *two* variables which are independent of each other, namely t and h, and must be expressed by $p = F(t, h)$. We notice at once that this function possesses, with regard to h, attributes which are quite analogous to those which it possesses in respect of t; it increases when h increases, but the surplus return from one worker for every hectare of land added is as certainly a decreasing magnitude as the surplus return from every new extension of production.

The yearly expenditure of capital, calculated for each worker, is here consequently $l + h \cdot r$, and equation (13) is now replaced by the equation

$$p = (l + h \cdot r)\left(1 + \frac{z \cdot t}{2}\right) \qquad (20)$$

which changes into (13) as soon as $r = 0$, that is to say, as soon as the use of land is supposed to be *free*.

Now thrift requires that at each level of wages and ground-rent the greatest possible capital interest should be attained. z must therefore become a maximum (l and r being assumed to be constant). As is well known, this is done by making its partial derivatives in respect of t and h, *each separately*, equal to zero. (That in this case a maximum is actually reached, can easily be proved by reference to the attributes of the function p indicated above.) Or we simply differentiate the above equation partially with regard to t and h, as if z, too, were a constant, and we obtain thereby the two new equations

$$\frac{dp}{dt} = (l + h . r) . \frac{z}{2} \tag{21}$$

and

$$\frac{dp}{dh} = r\left(1 + \frac{tz}{2}\right) \tag{22}$$

If, therefore, l and r were known, t, h and z could be determined from these three equations; so that we should obtain the most advantageous length of the period of production and the most profitable proportion of the use of land per worker, as well as the rate of interest itself, expressed in terms of wages and ground-rent.

But l and r, too, belong to the unknowns of the problem. To be able to solve it completely, we consequently need two independent equations as well. One of these is modelled on our previous equation (15). The existing capital of the community K must just suffice, in the case of the period of production and proportion of use of land in question, to employ fully all the available workers, and at the same time pay the necessary ground-rent. We therefore obtain, if the number of workers is A,

$$K = \frac{t}{2} . A . (l + h . r) \tag{23}$$

But just as all the available workers must here be employed by the capital, so, too, must *the whole of the available area of land*. If this is not the case, or if, on the contrary, more land is demanded than is available, the present level of ground-rent cannot be maintained; it must rise or fall, respectively. In other

words, when equilibrium is to be attained, the most advantageous proportion of the use of land per worker, found above,
must be equal to *the* proportion in which the number of hectares
of land existing within the whole economy stands to the existing
number of workers. If we express the former magnitude by B,
we consequently obtain as the required fourth equation simply

$$h = \frac{B}{A} \tag{24}$$

The problem is now solved in its entirety.

Equation (23) can in this case, of course, also be replaced by

$$K = \frac{t}{2}(Al + B \cdot r) \tag{23*}$$

The existing capital must suffice to pay all the workers during
the period of production adopted, and must at the same time
be sufficient to rent the whole of the land.

The landowners who work with their own means are here
conceived in the double role of capitalists and landowners,
just as, in the foregoing, we have treated the workers who are
themselves capitalists. All three functions can, of course, be
united in one person.

Discussion of the equations set forth above would now
reveal the true relationship between capital-interest, wage and
ground-rent—in so far as the assumptions which we have made
are in approximate agreement with reality.[1]

[1] In passing, we may show that what Böhm-Bawerk has to say about the
influence of ground-rent on capital-interest can scarcely be right.

Böhm-Bawerk asserts (loc. cit., p. 438) that the advance of capital to landowners (ground-rent) has an effect on the level of the rate of interest precisely
analogous to the effect of the existence of the consumption loan (discussed by
him before). 'The fact that the landowners, too, compete for consumption loans,'
he continues, 'takes a portion of the means of subsistence out of the market,
and a result of this is that the investment of capital in production decreases;
investment must call a halt at a higher level of surplus returns; and in this way
the rate of interest is at last maintained on a higher level.'

But Böhm-Bawerk forgets the tremendous difference which is made by the
fact that the applicants for consumption loans pay interest on the advance of
capital which has been made to them, whilst the landowners do not. In other
words, *the portion of capital paid out as ground-rent together with the portion of
capital used in the production itself* (paid out as wages) *yields interest in the form
of the net profit of production.* Consequently it is not enough that the capital
diminished by ground-rent remains 'at a higher level of surplus returns.' When
in these circumstances the rate of interest is forced up, the case examined above
must occur, where (leaving out of account the services of the land) an increase

Just as the equations set forth above constitute a completion of Böhm-Bawerk's theory of interest, so they also include, as I shall now show, the older (Ricardo–Thünen) theory of ground-rent as a special case.

Our conditional equations obviously remain unchanged if, assuming in the first place *any two* of the three magnitudes *l*, *r* and *z* to be constant, we try to determine *t* and *h* in such a way that the third of these quantities becomes a maximum. If, therefore, we assume that *z* is constant and, in the meantime, for the sake of simplicity, = zero (or, which is the same, if we assume that its amount is already included in *l* and *r*), and if, moreover, we make the assumption that the length of the period of production is *unchangeable*, then equation (21) drops out and instead of (20) and (22) we obtain simply

$$\begin{cases} p = l + h \cdot r \\ \dfrac{dp}{dh} = r \end{cases}$$

The former equation means that the yearly production of one worker must replace his yearly wage and, in addition, the ground-rent of the area of land which he has used. The latter equation, in its turn, expresses the fact that production will develop in the most advantageous way when each worker disposes of just so many hectares of land that the addition of a further hectare would increase his yearly production merely by the amount of the ground-rent of this hectare; since the wage reaches its highest possible level if the ground-rent is unchanged, and, vice versa, if the wage is unchanged, the ground-rent per hectare reaches the highest possible level.

In order to show that this is nothing else but the ordinary

of productive capital would lead to an absolutely lower net profit and a *decrease* of capital would consequently yield an absolutely *greater* net profit. That this is really the case in the present state of production, is scarcely credible. It seems to me most probable that if ground-rent were abolished, that is to say, if the services of the land were free, capitalists would obtain a *higher* interest on their capital. But what would happen if—as Böhm-Bawerk supposes by way of example—the taxation of ground-rent reached a confiscatory level or private ownership of land were even abolished, is less easy to decide. Actually, however, ground-rent would *not* be abolished, but would be paid by the capitalists exactly as before; only the state would have replaced the private owner of landed property.

theory of ground-rent, we choose as unit for the used area of land, instead of one hectare only, an area so great that on each of these area-units a large number of workers can be employed. Our h then becomes a proper fraction; indeed, $\frac{1}{n}$, if n stands for the number of workers employed per unit of area. In the same way, $p = \frac{q}{n}$, when q stands for the yearly production attained by the unit of land. Although n is here a *whole* number according to the nature of the matter, it can be treated approximately as a continuous magnitude. Thus we obtain, according to the rules of the differential calculus,

$$\frac{dp}{dh} = \frac{d\frac{q}{n}}{d\frac{1}{n}} = q - n\frac{dq}{dn}$$

and the above-mentioned system of equations turns into

$$\begin{cases} q = nl + r \\ q - n\dfrac{dq}{dn} = r \end{cases}$$

or into

$$\begin{cases} q = nl + r \\ \dfrac{dq}{dn} = l \end{cases}$$

which is the same thing.

What these two equations provide is precisely the mathematical expression of Ricardo's theory of rent in the form given to it by Thünen. The significance of the first equation is self-evident (here, of course, r stands for the ground-rent of the *present* area-unit). But the second equation expresses the fact that the most advantageous production is attained if on each area-unit just so many workers are employed that the employment of a further worker would yield *merely his annual wage* and no more; which agrees with Thünen's well-known law, mentioned above.

If we wish to take into consideration capital-interest as well here, we have simply to multiply the right side of the equations by $\left(1 + \dfrac{tz}{2}\right)$. But t must here be assumed to be a *constant*, otherwise a third relation is necessary, namely equation (21)[1], which now turns into

$$\frac{dq}{dt} = (nl + r) \cdot \frac{z}{2}$$

Now in the older theory of ground-rent the last relation was missing—quite naturally, since the length of the period of production has never been laid down as an independent concept. For this reason, however, the whole theory remained a very incomplete one. Without more exact definitions, there was talk of different quantities of 'labour and capital' or of different 'doses' of capital which are added to the land successively. But labour and capital can be used in various ways, and in particular it makes an important difference whether the capital is used simply to employ several workers in direct production, or for preparatory work, production of machines, breeding of draught-animals and food-producing animals, etc., as well—in other words, whether a longer or shorter period of production is adopted. Altogether, one could never arrive at the necessary factors which determine the level of capital-interest without considering this circumstance, and for the relationship between capital and wages there was, after all, only the completely insufficient wage fund theory. In all these respects Böhm-Bawerk's theory forms, so to speak, the corner-stone which before was missing. Once this corner-stone had been laid, the science of economics could be looked on as something complete in itself.

All rent-goods (buildings, railways, etc.) which form, each

---

[1] At the very beginning, of course, we could equally well have set down the equation

$$q = (nl + r)\left(1 + \frac{tz}{2}\right)$$

and its derivatives in respect of t and n

$$\frac{dq}{dt} = (nl + r) \cdot \frac{z}{2} \quad \text{and} \quad \frac{dq}{dn} = l\left(1 + \frac{tz}{2}\right)$$

and combined them with equations (23*) and (24), which latter is to be replaced by $n = \dfrac{A}{B}$.

However, we have preferred to use as starting-point the production of one worker supported by the forces of nature.

group by itself, an unvarying sum of goods (assuming a stationary economy), would, in my opinion, have to be treated in the same way as landed property. In this case, of course, a special unit would have to be chosen for each group. However, I will not dwell on this matter, but will at once proceed to show how, with the help of the theory of capital-interest and ground-rent which we have obtained, our problem of the exchange values of goods, which we left for the time being at the end of the previous chapter, can now be treated in an exact way.

6—Attempt at a definite theory of the value of goods. Criticism of Walras's presentation

Let us first of all try to imagine what an economy must be like, if the equations (20)–(24) (or the alternative equations given in the footnote to p. 152) are to reflect the *true* play of economic phenomena. This requires, of course, that within the whole economy only one single consumption good, for instance corn, is produced. Wages, ground-rent and capital-interest are all received in the form of goods, that is to say, in corn, and the capital itself consists of corn and the installations and tools necessary for the production of corn, which, however, we imagine as being so simple that they can be produced by the economies in question themselves and are of short duration. Durable goods are not produced at all. The economy must be a completely stationary one.

Let us now suppose that *beside* this economy there exists another, where in the same way another commodity—again, a single commodity only; for instance, linen—is produced. Exchange between the two economies is completely free, but capital and labour *cannot* be transferred from one to the other. For each of these two economies there would then exist a system of equilibrium equations similar to system (20)–(24). The constants of the equations—the number of workers, the area of land and the capital—as well as the form of the function of productivity p (or q) are, however, different for both economies. Let the above-mentioned magnitudes be A_1, B_1, K_1 and p_1 for one economy and A_2, B_2, K_2 and p_2 for the other. When these magnitudes are inserted in equations (20)–(24) instead of A, B, K and p, we obtain from each of these equilibrium systems, by elimination of the remaining unknowns,[1] first the length of the period of production t in question, then the values of the magnitudes l, r and z which we require to know. If these values are t_1, l_1, r_1 and z_1 for the first economy and t_2, l_2, r_2 and z_2 for the second, then $A_1 l_1 + B_1 r_1 + K_1 z_1$ and $A_2 l_2 + B_2 r_2 + K_2 z_2$ respectively express the quantities of goods which are produced every year in the two economies. Since, furthermore, the distribution of capital property and landed property within each economy must be assumed to be constant, we know now how much of this production falls to each person's share. Of these quantities of goods, one part of the yearly production of one economy is exchanged for one part of the yearly production of the other economy. And this exchange takes place exactly according to the laws of exchange developed previously. If, for instance, some proportion of exchange (the price on both sides) is first of all assumed at random, then each of the owners of corn—that is to say, each worker, landowner and capitalist of the first economy—offers, at this price, a certain quantity of the corn which has fallen to his share for the year in exchange for a corresponding quantity of linen—i.e. just so much that the ratio of the marginal utilities of corn and linen (appropriate to the quantities of corn and linen which have been consumed during the year) is made equal to the ratio of the prices, that is, the proportion of exchange. By addition of these partial quantities, we obtain the yearly supply of corn and the yearly demand for linen on the part of the owners of corn—at the price in question. In exactly the same way a total supply of linen and a total demand for corn arise on the other side, at the same price. If supply of, and demand for, the one commodity are equal, and consequently also equal with regard to the other commodity, equilibrium is attained; if not, a shifting of prices must take place. *But this change has obviously no influence on the proportion of production on both sides.* The problem of international trade, of which we have here presented the simplest pattern, is therefore, in fact, much less complicated than that of internal trade. Before long an average proportion of exchange

---

[1] This elimination can be done quite easily for l, r and z (even without knowing the form of the function of p). h is then replaced simply by $\dfrac{B}{A}$ in equations (20), (21) and (22).

will establish itself. Afterwards, this proportion is maintained practically unaltered from year to year, and is characterized by the fact that for *every* member of both economies the proportionality between marginal utility and price of both commodities is fulfilled. In this case, of course, it is not necessary that each individual member should appear in the exchange market. Without essential change in the proportions, the exchange can be transacted by all the capitalists, or by a few of them; so that wage, ground-rent and capital-interest, too, can be paid in both kinds of goods or in any conventional medium of exchange (for instance, paper money), provided only the above-mentioned proportion of marginal utility is thereby realized as the final result.

But if we now imagine that both economies are united *in a single economy*, so that the existing workers, natural resources and capitals of both can now be used indiscriminately in the one or the other production of goods, then at first sight everything seems fluid. If we wish to make use of two equilibrium systems here, the difficulty arises that the magnitudes A_1, A_2, B_1, B_2, K_1, K_2 can no longer be assumed to be known; to begin with, we only know the sums $A_1 + A_2 = A$; $B_1 + B_2 = B$. As for the capitals K_1 and K_2, neither they themselves nor their sum are known, strictly speaking. The national capital, in so far as it is free, consists here of *two* commodities, and its value can therefore only be determined after having found out their prices—that is to say, can only be expressed in one of these or in some other conventional medium of exchange.

But, on the other hand, it is obvious that in this case two different rates of wage, rates of rent and rates of interest can no longer exist, but wage, rent and interest on both sides will become approximately equal (in so far as the labour force and natural resources can be assumed to be uniform).

Let us first try to give an account of *how* these changes would come about after abolition of the boundary-line between the two economies. Let us suppose that at first l_1 and l_2, r_1 and r_2, z_1 and z_2 are still different. If $l_1 > l_2$, the workers will gradually go over from the linen business to the corn business: A_1 increases; A_2, on the other hand, decreases. And vice versa: if, when the boundary-line is abolished, r_1, for instance, is smaller than r_2, part of the land used for the cultivation of corn will gradually be employed for the production of linen. B_1

decreases and B_2 increases. Finally, if z_1, for instance, is at first smaller than z_2, the capital engaged in the production of corn, in proportion as it becomes *free* (which occurs by production itself), will be partly invested in the production of linen. Since this capital appears first in the form of corn, some of the workers in the linen business will consequently, if no account is taken of previous exchanges, now receive their wages directly in corn. However, this does not make any difference to them, provided the proportion of exchange between linen and corn remains unchanged. But this proportion of exchange cannot remain unaffected by the changes which have taken place either. If, therefore, taking corn as the standard of value, the price of linen has fallen, the capitalists, whose free capital consists mainly of linen, must increase the number of pieces in their capital stock if they wish to restore to it the same value; if, on the contrary, the price has risen, they can, without loss, decrease this number and consume part themselves. But it is very probable that *all* the capitalists will increase the number of pieces in their capital stock, at least for some time. In general, this freer and therefore more appropriate employment of productive forces must necessarily lead to higher productivity within both branches of business, and this increased productivity will facilitate the formation of new capital, until finally the stationary situation is again reached— only this time with more capital and probably a higher average level of ground-rent and wages (but not necessarily a higher average level of the *rate of interest*).

To pursue all these changes in detail is quite impossible, especially as they take place in an infinite number of different ways. We can, however, determine without difficulty the position of equilibrium finally attained, with the help of our equations set forth above—but only if we assume that the present capital is a known magnitude.

First of all the two initial equations

$$p_1 = (l + h_1 r)\left(1 + \frac{t_1 z}{2}\right); \quad p_2 = (l + h_2 r)\left(1 + \frac{t_2 z}{2}\right)$$

with their derivatives[1] in respect of t_1, h_1, t_2 and h_2 (altogether six equations), must be fulfilled.

The magnitudes l, r and z are now equal on both sides. On

---

[1] Analogous to equations (21) and (22).

the other hand, we assume here for each branch of the business, according to the nature of things, a special form of the productivity function $p = F(t,h)$ (which we assume to be known), as well as a different length of the most profitable period of production and a different proportion of the use of land (number of hectares per worker or, vice versa, number of workers per hectare). We therefore have, for the time being, six independent equations with the seven unknowns t_1, t_2, h_1, h_2, l, r and z.

In the equations still remaining

$$h_1 = \frac{B_1}{A_1}; \quad h_2 = \frac{B_2}{A_2}$$

$$K_1 = \frac{t_1}{2}(A_1 l + B_1 r); \quad K_2 = \frac{t_2}{2}(A_2 l + B_2 r)$$

the six new unknowns A_1, A_2, B_1, B_2, K_1 and K_2 occur, but for their determination we still have the equations

$$A_1 + A_2 = A$$
$$B_1 + B_2 = B$$
$$K_1 + K_2 = K$$

where A, B and K stand for the number of workers, area of land and capital existing within the whole economy, the latter expressed in terms of corn. We therefore have altogether thirteen equations with the same number of unknowns,[1] *but only on the assumption that the proportion of exchange of both commodities is known.*

Here, p_1 and p_2 express *values*, that is to say, they give the exchange value of the yearly production (as functions of t and h). But, of course, in the first instance only the number or quantity of the products in question is, in fact, established by the functions of productivity, which were assumed to be known on both sides. Since now the corn has been taken as our standard of value, p_1—the value of the production of corn (per

---

[1] The unknowns which were introduced last can, it is evident, be eliminated very easily. By this means we obtain between t_1, t_2, h_1, h_2, l and r and between the known magnitudes A, B and K one single relation, namely

$$K = \frac{1}{2(h_1 - h_2)}\{t_1(h_2 A - B)(l + h_1 r) - t_2(h_1 A - B)(l + h_2 r)\}$$

which in conjunction with the first six equations, is sufficient for the determination of the still remaining unknowns t_1, t_2, h_1, h_2, l, r and z.

year and worker)—is dependent merely on t_1 and h_1; the function p_2, on the other hand, includes, in so far as it is supposed to give the exchange value of the production of linen, another factor π, namely the proportion of exchange of both commodities or the uniform price of linen expressed in terms of corn.[1] But this proportion of exchange cannot be assumed to be known here; rather, our task is to show how it is determined by the interplay of all the economic forces. We therefore still have one unknown in excess of the number of equations and need one more of the above-mentioned independent equations, if the problem is to be completely solved.

To find this, we must imagine ourselves placed on the market of exchange of both commodities, and we must lay down the condition that on this market, too, there is equilibrium—equilibrium between supply and demand or, what is here the same, equilibrium between production and consumption.

This can come about, for instance, in the following way. At each level of l, r and z the yearly income of every single member of the economy, in addition to other factors, is definitely fixed. If, for instance, the individual in question is a worker himself, and if he possesses b hectares of land and has invested in the production capital of the value k, then his yearly income e is expressed by $e = l + br + kz$. This income he uses, according to our fundamental assumption, to the last penny (or rather to the last part of corn) for his yearly consumption of corn and linen. We therefore obtain

$$e = x + \pi y$$

when x and y respectively stand for his yearly consumption of these goods.[2] But these quantities must now fulfil the law of marginal utility, so that, if $f(\ )$ and $g(\ )$ stand for the marginal utility functions related to the quantity of the yearly consumption,

$$f(x) : g(y) = 1 : \pi$$

Since the forms of the functions $f(\ )$ and $g(\ )$ must be assumed to be known, x and y can be determined from the last two

[1] When $q_2 = F(t_2, h_2)$ expresses the number of pieces of linen produced (per year and worker), then $p_2 = \pi . q_2 = \pi . F(t_2, h_2)$.

[2] It is in this case totally indifferent in what form he originally receives his income, whether in the form of corn or linen or both, since linen is always expressed, at the equilibrium price π, in terms of corn.

equations, that is to say, can be expressed in terms of l, r, z and π. When this operation is carried through for each member of the economy,[1] we have also found the total consumption of, or demand for, the goods concerned, and, according to what has been said above,

$$X = \Sigma x = A_1 p_1$$

The yearly consumption of corn on the part of the total economy must correspond to the yearly production of corn. In the same way, with regard to the consumption and production of linen,

$$Y = \Sigma y = A_2 \frac{p_2}{\pi}$$

One of these equations, however, can be derived from the other; for we obtain from these

$$A_1 p_1 + A_2 p_2 = \Sigma x + \pi \Sigma y = \Sigma e = Al + Br + Kz$$

On the other hand, as is evident, we obtain by addition of our initial equations of production, or by multiplying them by A_1 and A_2,

$$A_1 p_1 + A_2 p_2 = A_1(l + h_1 r)\left(1 + \frac{t_1 z}{2}\right) + A_2(l + h_2 r)\left(1 + \frac{t_2 z}{2}\right)$$

$$= Al + Br + Kz$$

The one or the other of the above equations gives us, consequently, the hitherto missing relation between our unknown magnitudes. If A_1 and A_2 are already eliminated, we can instead use the equation

$$\frac{X}{p_1} + \frac{\pi \cdot Y}{p_2} = A_1 + A_2 = A$$

Or we could imagine each of the two branches of production as complete in itself, so that the yearly production is in the first instance simply distributed among the members as wage, rent and interest, and the supplies on both sides are partly exchanged later. p_1 as well as p_2 are then to be thought of as numbers of pieces. Wage and rent, likewise expressed in terms

[1] It is clear that, if a really numerical treatment of the problems should ever be attempted, the consumers would have to be divided into larger groups, whose consumption of, or demand for, the various goods could be found out empirically at each level of prices.

of number of pieces of the commodity in question, are connected by the relations

$$l_1 = \pi l_2, \quad r_1 = \pi r_2$$

and if the capital invested on both sides is in the first instance valued in terms of the commodities concerned, then

$$K_1 + \pi K_2 = K$$

in which K, as before, expresses the known value of the total national capital (valued in corn). If now, for instance, the individual mentioned above uses b_1 hectares in the corn business and b_2 in the linen business, or invests the capitals k_1 and k_2 and has himself worked about eight months in the corn business and four months in the linen business, then he receives each year

and
$$\tfrac{2}{3}l_1 + b_1 r_1 + k_1 z \text{ corn}$$
$$\tfrac{1}{3}l_2 + b_2 r_2 + k_2 z \text{ linen}$$

All these individual quantities are then brought to the corn–linen market and are partly exchanged against each other. The equilibrium price, found according to the rules of exchange, appears now as a known function of l_1, l_2, r_1, r_2 and z, but must equal π, by which means the missing relation is found. Both methods, obviously, lead to the same result, and we can lay down as the final result of our investigation the rule:

If an economy comprises the production, distribution and consumption of only two commodities, the proportion of exchange between them is given by the following conditions: (1) that wage, rent and interest during production of both commodities must be equal; (2) that at the level of wages and rent attained, interest becomes a maximum (or, in general, at the attained level of two of these three magnitudes, the third becomes a maximum); (3) that the existing capital must just suffice to employ the existing number of workers and to rent the existing area of land, and; (4) that the two commodities are distributed among all members of the economy directly or after a preceding exchange, in such a way that the ratio of the marginal utilities of the quantities consumed yearly becomes everywhere equal to the ratio of exchange of the goods.

We have now reached the end of our investigation; for if the theory developed here has gone to the root of economic phenomena, all complications of the problem will find their solution by suitable combinations of equations of the kind laid down above, at least in so far as it is a question of a stationary economy. Let us glance at these complications as they occur in real economic life.

1. Production and consumption in a modern economy comprise not only two commodities, but hundreds of them, even if only the main kinds of goods are reckoned; and within every class of goods there is usually a large number of different qualities and specialities.

However, this circumstance will only make necessary a larger number of equations. With every new commodity which must be taken into consideration, six new unknowns enter the problem, according to our above-mentioned scheme; since for each commodity the most profitable period of production and proportion of the use of land, the number of workers, area of land and capital employed in its production, and finally the exchange value of the commodity are to be determined. If there are n goods and one of them is taken as the standard of value, the number of unknowns will consequently be $6n + 2$.[1] For their determination the *laws of production* give, as can easily be seen, $5n + 3$ independent equations, whilst the missing $n - 1$ equations are obtained from the *laws of exchange* —for instance, by means of a formula expressing the fact that, at the $n - 1$ prices of the goods, which must be determined and expressed in terms of one of them, the quantity of each commodity yearly consumed or demanded must be equal to its yearly production, and by taking into consideration that only $n - 1$ of the n equations laid down in this way are independent.[2]

2. Labour and forces of land were each assumed as a homogeneous mass.

This is, of course, not correct. For certain productions there is at any time only a very limited number of workers who are employable at all, since the business requires either special

[1] Namely $t_1 \ldots t_n$, $h_1 \ldots h_n$, $A_1 \ldots A_n$, $B_1 \ldots B_n$, $K_1 \ldots K_n$, the l's, r's and z's for all productions, and finally the $n - 1$ proportions of exchange— independent of each other—of the n goods. In the way indicated on p. 132, footnote 1, the $3n$ magnitudes $A_1 \ldots A_n$, $B_1 \ldots B_n$, $K_1 \ldots K_n$ can easily be eliminated, and in this way the number of the unknowns of the problem is reduced to $3n + 2$.

[2] When in this case two or more goods can partly replace each other, the marginal utility of any one of them will, of course, not only be a function of the yearly consumed quantity of *this* commodity, but of all the goods in question.

abilities or a longer training. In order that this circumstance may be taken into consideration, the existing workers must be divided into groups, and the wage for each group, which can then be very different for the various groups, must be ascertained separately. But once the boundary-lines of these groups are drawn, the number of independent conditioning equations (*Bedingungsgleichungen*) will here obviously increase also to the same extent as the number of the unknowns.[1]

As for natural resources, we come first of all to the well-known fact of the difference of landed property with regard to fertility, situation, etc. But, in addition to this, there are natural resources of an entirely different kind: agricultural landed property, fish-ponds, woods, ore-bearing tracts, waterfalls, etc. For each of these kinds, a special uniform measure must, of course, be chosen.

Finally, in my opinion, produced goods also, in so far as they are continuing sources of rent, should be taken into consideration here. In the stationary economy such goods are not produced at all, but kept in the same good condition.[2] The capital investment in question itself belongs to past time and need no longer be considered. The net interest on this capital has consequently the precise character of a rent, since necessary repairs and maintenance work, as well as running costs, are imposed on the capitalist who uses these goods.

On the other hand, it cannot be right to do as Böhm-Bawerk does and try to exclude means of improving the soil, as soon as they have 'grown together' with the land, from the sphere of capital. In the same way, improvements, such as fertilization and the like, which suffice for only a few harvests and must consequently replace the invested capital after a short time, belong obviously to agriculturally-employed capital in the

[1] If workers from the different groups are employed in the same production, the equations in question become, of course, even more complicated, especially as the proportion of workers of different categories would often have to be ascertained according to the principle of the greatest possible profit (difference between male, female and young workers, etc.). Similarly with regard to different qualities of land and to rent-goods altogether.

[2] The replacement of completely worn out goods of this kind by new ones need not be excluded, of course, but can be regarded as repair of a greater complex of goods. According to the conception stated above, the difference between rent-goods and capital-goods consists in the fact that the sum of the former is *independent* of the length of the period of production of consumption goods.

narrower sense, as do tools, labour, draught animals and food-producing animals, etc.

Dwelling-houses, too, must in my opinion be added to rent-goods. Dwellings—just as much as food, clothes, heating, etc.—belong to the needs which must be satisfied from the economic point of view. Why, then, should the service of giving shelter which dwelling-houses provide not be put in the same category as the economic services of fields, meadows, woods, fish-ponds, etc.? From the point of view of the *stationary* economy there is scarcely any substantial difference left between them.

The boundary-line between rent-goods and capitals in the narrower sense can, I grant, only be established empirically, and even then only approximately. Practically, however, the difference is a highly important one. The volume of circulating capital determines the level of wage, rent and capital-interest. Upon these the highly durable goods merely exercise the same influence as, say, the size of the cultivated area of land. But their *capital* value is, at least in the stationary economy, an entirely secondary phenomenon and has for the exchange values of consumable goods no importance whatsoever.

For production, we have consequently to consider—once this boundary-line is drawn—not merely the capital K and the different groups of workers A^I, A^{II}, A^{III}, A^{IV}, etc., but also the different groups of rent-goods B^I, B^{II}, B^{III}, B^{IV}, etc., each with its different quantity-unit and rent of this unit. Each new group becomes the source of new unknowns but also the source of the necessary number of new independent equations.

3. It was assumed that the production of a new commodity in all its different stages is done in one single business. In reality this is practically never the case. The raw materials and means of production are usually produced in special firms; the same factory often supplies tools and machines for several different branches of business, and, on the other hand, half-finished products and raw materials coming from quite different sources are put together and further worked up in a single business, etc. Viewed prospectively or retrospectively, the businesses branch out or meet.

This circumstance would create no special difficulties if the production of each separate commodity could be followed through the various businesses, and if we could find out what quantity of labour, capital and natural resources (or of services of the other rent-goods) has been engaged in the completion of this particular commodity. If this is not possible, and if, consequently, the production of two or more commodities forms more or less an indissoluble whole, then, if we are to treat the problem mathematically, these goods must be united in one single group; because then they pay for the labour, capital and rent-goods used in their production not separately, but all together. In the equations of *exchange*, however, they are to be treated separately again (in so far as two or more of them cannot replace each other).

4. The supply of labour was treated as a constant magnitude. This is not quite correct even if the number of workers remains the same; for the daily working-time can, in certain circumstances, vary, or several days or weeks of the year can be spent in idleness—not only because of lack of employment during certain seasons, but also because the worker may allow himself more leisure when wages are more abundant. That is to say, a labourer's ability to work or his time, unlike most rent-goods, is of value to its possessor, even when it is not used productively.

If, therefore, we do not (with L. Walras) use the word 'production' in such a general sense that even a person's use of his spare time, a walk, etc., is regarded and treated as 'production,' it obviously becomes necessary to consider the yearly working-time, and consequently the yearly production, of a worker as itself a function of the wage. It must be remarked in this connexion, however, that, even if the working-time of the individual worker possibly decreases when wages rise, yet, on the other hand, people who have previously lived in idleness are now tempted or rather forced by the higher price of labour to become workers themselves. Moreover, men will be able to work harder in the shorter working-time because of the greater abundance of food, etc. It cannot therefore be decided *a priori* to what extent, in given circumstances, a rise or fall in wages would increase or reduce the effective supply of labour. Each individual case must be investigated separately.

5. Finally, our assumption of a stationary economy represents only the simplest case which is theoretically conceivable, but which never quite comes to pass in reality. In exceptional cases, such as our own century, for instance, there can even occur a

progression of society so great that this hypothesis does not correspond even approximately to reality. In any case the theory must, in order to be complete, not only be able to treat the statics but also the dynamics of economic phenomena; it must not only take into consideration the equilibrium of economic forces, but also the disturbance of this equilibrium caused by their changes.

The number of workers, or, more generally, of the population, can be increased by a rise in the birth rate or by immigration, and can be decreased by exceptionally heavy mortality or by emigration. The sum of rent goods, including the cultivated area of land, can be increased by industry and decreased by neglect respectively. Lastly, the national income can suffer changes in several ways. *The transformation of capital in the narrower sense into rent-goods* or even *into working ability* (its sacrifice for purposes of education) is here to be emphasized as such a change, and, what is more, as a change of the greatest importance.

If in all these relationships a certain *rate* of progression may be assumed to be given, then it is clear that equations of production and exchange can be laid down. We have then, so to speak, a problem of dynamic equilibrium instead of a problem of static equilibrium with which to deal.[1]

It would be quite a different matter to try to lay down laws for determining the rate of progression itself. I personally make no attempt in this direction.[2] How far present-day political economy still is from being able to treat these situations in an exact way, becomes clear if we consider the fact that economists are still by no means agreed as to the extent to which such a

[1] The production of new rent-goods, for instance, must then be treated in the same way as the production of consumable goods, in which case, however, the sum of the circulating capital no longer remains unchanged. Instead, the condition is added that the newly produced rent-goods must yield as rent the usual capital-interest on the costs of production.

[2] We could, of course—as L. Walras does—think of the yearly savings, and consequently the increase of capital, under otherwise unchanging circumstances, as *a function of the level of interest*, provided we keep in mind that a rise in the rate of interest can not only give cause for an increase in savings, but can also, in certain circumstances, have the contrary effect, and vice versa. But then the population must necessarily be assumed to be stationary or at least its yearly change must be assumed to be given; for obviously—to take an example—the number of children in a family is of much greater importance for the eventual formation or consumption of capital by that family, than the level of the rate of interest.

progression of society is advantageous or not. In particular, so far as I know, the question has never been raised in economic writings, what size of population is economically most profitable when the amount of capital, size of the area of land, etc., are given. If, therefore, these problems are to be solved according to the principle of the greatest utility, it is obviously a serious drawback that there is not even common agreement *in what direction* economic advantage or disadvantage in fact lies. If, on the other hand, we assume that changes of population are not regulated according to the principle of what is economically most advantageous (in the widest sense of the word), but are regulated now and for ever merely by blind natural instincts, then at least we are on firm ground. In that case, however, we should have no alternative but to accept Ricardo's doctrine of the natural wage—that is to say, the smallest possible wage—as a fact beyond dispute. Altogether, population questions are unfortunately still neglected by the economists of practically *all* schools. This is regrettable from the theoretical point of view, but still more regrettable, of course, from the practical point of view.

Even if we take no account of the unfortunate state of affairs last mentioned and look at the problem as a purely statical one, the foregoing enumeration shows that the list of complications is a very considerable one. But it is clear, when treating concrete problems of reality, as soon as the required facts are more or less at hand, all necessary simplifications will follow automatically. The practical business man has, after all, to consider as far as possible all circumstances which influence the conditions of production and sale of his commodity. If he cannot possibly penetrate, or does not need to see at a glance, *all* phenomena of the market, this may be regarded as proof that, for the theoretical treatment of the problems which he has in fact to solve, at first only a comparatively small number of the pertinent magnitudes need be inserted in the calculation.

Above all, we should, in this case, have to define more precisely the still somewhat hazy concept of the length of the period of production within the individual main businesses— for instance, agriculture, the textile industry, the iron industry, etc.—and to find out the increase in this period which has resulted from the improvements introduced from time to time, in so far as they have really required a larger investment of capital. Once such information is available for the main fields of economic life, the counting procedure and, with it, the *a posteriori* investigation of the theory can start. It must be remembered, however, that the results of the theory can only remain valid on the assumption of completely free competition.

The doctrine set forth here has much in common with the theory presented in Léon Walras's *Élements d'économie politique pure*. There, too, equations of production are laid down and combined with the equations of exchange previously obtained. But, as was remarked above, Walras calls 'capital' and treats as 'capital' *only* durable goods, but not raw materials and half-finished products and not the means of subsistence of workers. What the owner of the circulating capital advances to the workers, landowners, etc., is therefore not treated by Walras as capital at all. It is therefore implicitly assumed by Walras that workers and other producers maintain themselves during production and receive remuneration for their productive services from the proceeds of the products in question only after completion of the production. This is obviously incorrect. In this interpretation the true rôle of capital in production is completely overlooked. A necessary consequence of this is the peculiar fact that these equations of production and exchange *can give no information at all about the level of the rate of interest*. If only durable goods are regarded as capital, then a certain *rent* is fixed for each group of these by the above-mentioned equations, but *not* the *capital value* of the goods itself, nor, consequently, the *rate* of interest either, 'le taux du revenu net.' This is explicitly admitted by Walras; but he asserts that, in order to determine the level of interest, it is necessary to turn from the investigation of a stationary economy to the investigation of a progressive one, where *new* interest-bearing capital goods are produced, whose capital value can be determined from the production costs. This is certainly incorrect. In the stationary economy, too—even if we assume that all the means of production are indestructible—a rate of interest of the circulating capital will undoubtedly establish itself, precisely because the lengthier methods of production prove more profitable. Walras's theory of production and capital consequently rests upon incorrect assumptions and cannot be regarded as definitive. However much it may—in several respects—testify to its author's acuteness, the real essence of the matter has not become clear to him. The merit of having taken the decisive step forward belongs in this field to Jevons and, above all, to Böhm-Bawerk.[1]

[1] In the second edition of his work, Walras, commenting on Böhm-Bawerk's theories, raises the objection that capital-interest can only establish itself *on the market* and that he has tried in vain to find mention of this market in Böhm-Bawerk's writings. Walras probably knows only the extract from Böhm-Bawerk's book in the *Revue d'économie politique* which he mentions, because it is precisely this market which is presented in sketches in the last chapter of the *Positive Theorie des Kapitals*, although the services of the land are left unconsidered. I have tried, in what has been said above, to supply what was wanting here.

BIBLIOGRAPHY

of Knut Wicksell's published works

By ARNE AMUNDSEN

This bibliography has been prepared with the aid of the source material available in the Oslo libraries. The works are listed, in chronological order, under the following headings:

I. Wicksell's main publications.
II. Articles and comments by Wicksell in *Ekonomisk Tidskrift*, 1899–1925.
III. Articles and reviews by Wicksell in journals, yearbooks, etc. (excluding *Ekonomisk Tidskrift*).
IV. Reviews by Wicksell in *Ekonomisk Tidskrift*.
V. Pamphlets by Wicksell (including some newspaper articles and public lectures).

I. Wicksell's Main Publications

1893 *Über Wert, Kapital und Rente nach den neueren nationalökonomischen Theorien*, Jena, 1893, xvi + 143 pp. A reprint, in German, was published in 1933 by The London School of Economics, as No. 15 in 'Series of Reprints of Scarce Tracts in Economic and Political Science.' English edition, 1953: *Value, Capital and Rent*, with a foreword by G. L. S. Shackle, translated by S. H. Frowein.

1895 *Zur Lehre von der Steuerincidenz*, Doktor-specimen, part one of *Finanztheoretische Untersuchungen*.

1896 *Finanztheoretische Untersuchungen nebst Darstellung und Kritik des Steuerwesens Schwedens*, Jena, 1896.

1898 *Geldzins und Güterpreise, eine Studie über die den Tauschwert des Geldes bestimmenden Ursachen*, Jena, 1898. English edition, 1936: *Interest and Prices*, with a foreword by Bertil Ohlin, translated by R. F. Kahn.

1901 *Föreläsningar i nationalekonomi*, part one. Lund, 1901. Second revised edition in Swedish, Lund, 1911. German edition, 1913. *Vorlesungen über Nationalökonomie auf Grundlage des Marginalprinzipes*,

Third Swedish edition, Lund, 1928.
English edition, 1934: *Lectures on Political Economy*, Volume One, 'General Theory,' with an introduction by Lionel Robbins, translated by E. Classen.
Fourth Swedish edition, Lund, 1938.

1906 *Föreläsningar i nationalekonomi*, part two. Lund, 1906. Summary in *Economic Journal*, 1907, vol. xvii, p. 213, under the title 'The Influence of the Rate of Interest on Prices' (lecture in the Economic Section of the British Association, 1906).
Second augmented edition, 1915.
German edition, 1922.
Third edition, Lund, 1928.
English edition, 1935: *Lectures on Political Economy*, Volume Two, 'Money.'
Fourth edition, Lund, 1937.

II. Articles and comments by Wicksell in *Ekonomisk Tidskrift*, 1899–1925

Year	Page	Title
1899	211–232	*Om öfverflytting av skatt.*
	383–387	*Ytterligare om öfverflytting av skatt.*
1900	305–337	*Om gränsproduktiviteten såsom grundval för den nationalekonomiska fördelningen.*
	12–49	*Rysslands ekonomiska förhållanden.*
1901	187–200	*Om afvecklingen af de äldre nyttjanderätterna à svenska statens skogar.*
	503–512	*Mjölkkor såsom dragare.*
	75–119	*Om arfsskatten.*
	423–434	*Om acker ur nationalekonomisk synpunkt.*
1902	424–433	*Till fördelningsproblemet.*
	543–550	*Professor Fahlbeck om nymalthusianismen.*
1903	485–507	*Den dunkla punkten i penningteorien.*
	340–347	*Jordbrukets produktionskostnader.*
	102–130	*Tyskland vid skiljovägen.*
1904	32–106	*Framtidens myntproblem.*
	457–474	*Mål och medel i nationalekonomien.*

Year	Page	Title
1907	41–52	*Knapps penningteori.*
	277–285	*Några felkällor vid försök till verifikation af lagen för jordens aftagande afkastning.*
1908	41–54	*En lektion i banklagstiftning.*
	207–214	*Penningvärdets stadgande, ett medel att förebygga kriser.*
	373–382	*Hvarför inskränkes fabriksdriften.*
1909	61–66	*Penningränta och varupris.*
1911	39–49	*Böhm-Bawerk kapitalteori och kritiken däraf.*
1912	43–48	*Tullar och arbetslöner.*
	309–322	*Kapital—und kein Ende.*
	432–433	*Monopolvinsten och dess beskattning jämte något om gross-och detaljhandelspris.*
	443–468	*Ålderdomsförsäkringskommittens betänkande.*
1913	134–142	*Penningvärdets reglerande.*
	211–217	*Resultatet.*
	224–227	*Anmärkningar till doc. Brocks Uppsats.*
1914	59–62	*Professurer i statistik.*
	75–84	*Dyrtid, tullar och arbetslöner.*
	123–126	Fritz Hüson Brock. Remark.
	126–127	Wicksell's rejoinder.
	195–208	*Kan ett land få för litet folk.*
	263–270	*Riksbankens guldkassa.*
	294–300	*Lexis och Böhm-Bawerk, I.*
	322–334	*Lexis och Böhm-Bawerk, II.*
1915	30–38	*Ekonomiska gåtor.*
	159–171	*Växelkurs och bankränta.*
	204–211	Victor Moll. Remark.
	353–357	*Nationalförmögenhet, nationalinkomst och "ärlige besparingar" i Tyskland.*
	364–368	*Frivilliga besparingar eller tvungna.*
1916	285–292	*Den "kritiska punkten" i lagen för jordbrukets aftagande produktivitet.*
	338–346	Remark by Rohtlieb.
	268–277	Remark by Davidson to an article (Wicksell's) in *Dagens Nyheter.*
	304–308	*Medel mot dyrtiden.* (Wicksell's rejoinder.)
	347–350	Davidson's rejoinder.

III. Articles and reviews by Wicksell in journals, yearbooks, etc. (excluding *Ekonomisk Tidskrift*)

1890 "Überproduktion—oder Überbevölkerung," *Zeitschrift für die gesamte Staatswissenschaft.*

1892 "Kapitalzins und Arbeitslohn," *Jahrbücher für National-ökonomie* 1892 (pp. 852–874). Summary in the same periodical, 1893.

1897 "Der Bankzins als Regulator der Warenpreise," *Jahrbücher für Nationalökonomie*, 1897 (pp. 228–243).

1898 "Penningräntans innflytande på varuprisen," *Nationalekonomiska Föreningens förhandlingar*, 1898, pp. 47–70.

1897 and 1899 Review of V. Pareto, *Cours d'économie politique*, in *Zeitschrift für Volkswirtschaft*.
My source is: *Ohlin*, in the *Economic Journal*, Sept. 1926, p. 512.

1907 "Krisernas gåta," *Statsøkonomisk Tidsskrift*, 1907.
"The Influence of the Rate of Interest on Prices," *Economic Journal*, 1907, vol. xvii, p. 213.

1909 "Über einige Fehlerquellen bei Verifikation des Bodengesetzes," *Thünen-Archiv*, 1909.
"Zur Verteidigung der Grenznutzenlehre," *Zeitschrift für die gesamte Staatswissenschaft, Social Tidsskrift*, 1909, pp. 97–102.

1913 Review of V. Pareto, *Manuel d'économic politique*, in *Zeitschrift für Volkswirtschaft*.

1917 Review of L. v. Mises, *Theorie des Geldes, und der Umlaufsmittel*, in *Zeitschrift für Volkswirtschaft*.

1916 "Hinauf mit den Bankraten," *Archiv für Sozialwissenschaft und Sozialpolitik*, 1916.

1918 "International Freights and Prices," *Quarterly Journal of Economics*, 1918.

IV. Reviews by Wicksell in *Ekonomisk Tidskrift*

Year	Page	Author and Title
1899	534–537	Gide, Charles: *Nationalekonomiens grunddrag.*
	462–469	*Klassisk nationalekonomi och vetenskapelig socialism.*
1902	85–90	Hobson, John A.: *The Economics of Distribution*, and Clark, John Bates: *The Distribution of Wealth. A Theory of Wages, Interest and Profits.*
1902	195–199	*Jordbruksarbetaren i Förenta staterna.*
1903	169–174	*Om begreppen produktivitet, rentabilitet och relativ afkastning inan jordbruket.*
1908	287–292	Spak, H. J.: *Landtarbetarfrågan I och II.*
1909	260–264	Aarum, Th.: *Arbeidets økonomiske værdi.*
	178–184	Wieth-Knudsen, K. A.: *Formerelse og Fremskridt.*

1915   230–233   *Finansiell krigsberedskap i Tyskland.*
         39–42   *Marknadsprisets inverkan på utlandet.*

1917   19–28   Brisman, Sven: *De moderna affärsbankerna.*
         393–397   Keilhau, Wilhelm: *Grundrentelæren.*
         309–311   *Penningränta och varupris* (remark in a discussion).
         320–321   *Goschen om växelhurserna* (a correction).

1918   66–75   Petander, K.: *Goda och dårliga tider.*
         134–137   *Grundrentelæren.* Rejoinder by Keilhau to Wicksell.
         138–140   *Genmäle.*

1920   124–125   *Frihandel och utvandring.*
         229   *Råvaruexport och utvandring—*II. Remark to Heckscher.

V. Pamphlets by Wicksell
(including some newspaper articles and public lectures)

1880   January or February, in a temperance society in Uppsala (opening a discussion). "Vilka äro de allmännaste orsakerna til dryckenskapslasten och huru kunna de undanrödjas?" Recorded in *Uppsalaposten.*
       25 February the same lecture was delivered to an academic society in Gillesalen, and was followed by a discussion in the newspapers, with contributions from Professor Davidson among others. The lecture has been printed.
       Svar til mina granskare, med ett tillägg om nymalthusianismens ställning och utsikter i Europa.

1881   Lecture in Stockholm and Uppsala: "Om utvandringen, dess betydelse och orsaker," published 1882 (?).

1887   *Om folkökningen i Sverige och de faror den medför för det allmänna välståndet och för sedeligheten,* with a preface dated London, October, 1887.

1890   *Om äktenskapet och dess framtid.*
       De sexuella frågorna, gransking av Hrr. Emil Svenséns, Bjørnstjerne Bjørnsons och professor Seved Ribbings broschyrer, with a postscript dated Paris, April, 1890.

1894 *Våra skatter, vilka betala dem, och vilka borde betala? Synspunkter och förslag av Sven Trygg*, Stockholm, 1894.

1909 "Läran om befolkningen," *Verdandi Småskrifter*, dated Ystad State Prison, October, 1909.

? *Die Grundzüge der modernen Werttheorie sowie der damals soeben erschienenen Böhm-Bawerkschen Theorie des Kapitals.*

INDEX

Agriculture, 38–9, 162
Amundsen, Arne, 13
Anderson, Dr., 38n.
Astronomy, 52
Auspitz, 20, 89–90
Austrian economists, 6, 8, 53
Average marginal utility, 74
Average wage, 141–2

Banking system, 8, 9, 11, 31
Bastiat, 17, 40, 41, 43
Bessemer, 42–3
Böhm-Bawerk, and agriculture, 162; his theory of capital, 23, 38, 40, 46, 97–8, 100, 101, 102, 103, 104, 105n.; his theory of capital-interest and wages, 53, 119, 120n., 123, 126, 128, 131; and capital goods, 118, 119; and the ground-rent, 146, 149n.; and interest, 21–2, 106–15, 133–5, 136, 142–4; mentioned, 5–6, 8, 17, 20, 168; and period of production, 10, 117, 119, 152; his theory of value, 48, 50; and wage fund theory, 145–6; and Walras, 168n.
Building sites, high values of, 42
Business cycle, 7, 12
Business man, and economic theory, 166

Cairnes, 29, 36
Calculus, 24
Canard, 52
Capital, Böhm-Bawerk's theory of, 5–6, 17, 21–3; concept of, 97–106; doses of, 152; fixed and variable, 145, 146; formation of, 21, 109, 116, 141, 156, 165n.; free, 156; and ground-rent, 147, 148, 149, 150n.; and harmony economists, 41–2; increasing, 139–41, 144; and interest, 104, 113, 142; kinds of, 105, 162–3; and labour, 23, 36–7, 126–7, 127–8, 132–3, 152; and land, 40–1n.; marginal efficiency of, 12; means of subsistence as, 101–3, 115, 144; new, 120; private and social, 100–5; and rent goods, 162, 165; role of, in production, 94, 110, 115–17, 121, 167; and period of production, 137, 138; productivity of, 110, 111, 113; as stored-up wealth, 98–9, 100, 101; use of outside business, 124; and Walras, 95–6, 167; and Wicksell, 9–10; per worker, 126

Capital-goods, 12, 99, 104n., 105, 106, 118–19, 162n., 167
Capital interest, Böhm-Bawerk's theory of, 21, 53, 119; and concept of capital, 106; and the market, 168n.; and period of production, 131, 132–3; theory of, 20, 94, 96, 117; and ground-rent, 24–5, 149, 151–2, 160; and wages, mathematical presentation, 120–30; see also Interest
Capitalism, and Ricardo, 35
Capitalists, and increasing capital, 139–41; as entrepreneurs, 127–8; means of subsistence of, 103–4; and period of production, 128–30; and workers, 98
Capital-labour market, 127, 136n.
Capital market, 98, 125
Capital profit, 36–7
Carey, 17, 111n.
Cartels, 70
Circulating capital, 96, 163, 165n., 167
Circulation of money, 9, 97
Claims, and capital, 104
Clark, J. B., 6
Coal industry, 41n., 98–9
Colonies, 109
Commodities, multiplicity of, 161
Community, enrichment of, 100
Comparative statics, 6
Competition, 36, 70, 94–5; see also Free competition
Compound interest, 122–3n., 142–3
Conditional equations, 150
Conrads Jahrbücher, 53n., 124n., 128
Consumable goods, as capital, 96, 98–9, 101, 102, 103–4, 105, 115; and interest, 106, 111–12, 113–14
Consumption, multiplicity of, 161; and production, 20, 158–9, 161; variation in, 82–3, 84–5
Consumption loans, 104, 107n., 114, 115n., 149n.
Continuous quantities, 62
Contract curve, 69
Corn, and supply and demand, 91
Costs, law of, 94
Credit, 77, 79n., 81

Debts, and capital, 104
Demand, and production, 93; see also Supply and demand
Demand curves, 87–9, 90, 91

THE END